FRANK LLOYD WRIGHT
A Retrospective View

FRANK LLOYD WRIGHT

A Retrospective View

Trewin Copplestone

Grange
BOOKS

Published in 1997 by
Grange Books
An imprint of Grange Books Plc.
The Grange,
Grange Yard.
London.
SE1 3AG

Printed in China

Jacket
Front: The Solomon R. Guggenheim Museum, New
            York, detail of the roof dome.
Back: Edgar J. Kaufmann Snr. House, 'Falling
            Water', Bear Run, Pennsylvania.

Pages 2-3   Taliesin West, Scottsdale, near Phoenix,
            Arizona.

Right   Living room of Falling Water, the Edgar J.
            Kaufmann Snr. House.

Photographic acknowledgements
Thomas A. Heinz Copyright ©. Pages 2-3, 4-5, 13, 14-15 all,
16, 17, 18, 19, 20, 22-23, 24, 25, 26, 27, 28-29 all, 30both, 31,
32, 33 all, 36 both, 37, 38-39 top and inset, 40-41 all, 42-43
both, 44-45 all, 48, 49 both, 50-51 all, 52 bottom, 52-53 top, 54-
55 both, 56 both, 57, 60, 61 both, 62-63 both, 64, 65 all, 66 top,
68 top, 69 all, 70-71 all, 72-73 all, 74-75, 76-77 and inset, 78-79
top, 96-97 all, 82-83, 84-85 bottom, 86-87, 88-89, 93 both, 94-
95 both, 96-97 and inset, 98, 99, 100-101 both, 102-103 both,
104-105, 106-107, 107, 110, 111. **Copyright © 1997 the Frank
Lloyd Wright Foundation, Scottsdale, Arizona.** Pages 28-29
top, 46 top and bottom, 47 top and bottom, 59, 78-79, 84-85 top.
**Courtesy The Frank Lloyd Wright Archives, Scottsdale,
Arizona.** Pages 11, 34, 45, 58. **Trewin Copplestone** Pages 10,
12 both, 19, 39 top right, 39 bottom left, 53 bottom both.
Florida Southern College. Pages 90, 91. **Angelo Hornak
Library.** Page 109. **Arcaid.** Pages 6, 108. **Courtesy of the
Trustees of the V & A Museum.** Page 79.

FRANK LLOYD WRIGHT 1867-1959

This book is about Frank Lloyd Wright. It is not the first, neither will it be the last. His work is of such significance and importance as to be worthy of regular evaluation and numerous books on the subject of his life and architecture have been written, including some by Wright himself. It is not unreasonable to ask why there should be yet another: what more is there to be said? There are many reasons why the work of important figures should attract constant reappraisal. New facts emerge, values change, perceptions of achievement alter. The Millennium seems a particularly appropriate time to evaluate the life and work of anyone who has made a significant contribution to society in this century. This is assuredly so in the case of Frank Lloyd Wright. He was born in 1867 but his most important work belongs firmly to this century where he remains the most significant among American-born architects.

Architecture, it should be remembered, is highly indicative of the character of any society and provides not only its most visible monuments but also determines to a considerable degree the patterns of our lives. It is not a take it or leave it product – we have to use architecture to live as we do. This point needs emphasizing because it establishes the actual importance of architects in conditioning all our lives. Since society demands change or changes involuntarily, architecture must also change and this lies in the hands of architects. Wright strongly believed in himself and his ability to design buildings, correspondingly positive, has been important in forming, in part, the character of 20th-century architecture.

This book is concerned, in consequence, with examining how far Wright, through his architecture and his influence, through his writings and lectures, had a beneficial or detrimental effect on architecture and attitudes towards architecture which have emerged through the century.

The new Millennium seems to demand retrospection and re-evaluation of the many achievements of the century. There is almost no area, it seems, unless it is in the field of human relationships, that great advances in technology have not been made which have and continue to have unimagined influence on the patterns of social behaviour.

When one reflects that the first controlled power flight by the Wright brothers, Orville and Wilbur, occurred on 17 December 1903 at Kitty Hawk in the United States when Frank Lloyd Wright (no relation) was 36 years old (and that only ten years after his death man had landed on the moon), and the degree to which the whole world now depends on air transport, one realizes that in this aspect of science at least, extraordinary advances have been made. Such energetic activity and inventive diversity was not confined to industrial and scientific advances. While all aspects of society and culture have seen similar dramatic developments, the matter of architectural advance has not always seemed so evident. Indeed, this century has witnessed great periods of dissension and acrimony and it still cannot be said that a consensus on the best way forward into the Millennium has been reached in terms of architectural design and town and city planning. This is, of course, not solely the responsibility of the architect.

There is one preliminary point to be made on the subject of the architect. Since the Renaissance, it is inevitable that works of art have come to be recognized and identified by the names of their creators; we always wish to know what name to attach to a work of art in order that we may use it as a basic measure of quality. The cult of personality feeds on the importance placed on this form of name value. Any retrospective view of the arts of this century will, in consequence, concentrate on the work of individuals. It is therefore appropriate in the last decade of this century to review the work of its greatest architects and attempt to make a balanced and accurate evaluation of their respective contributions.

Architecture is unusual among the fine arts in at least two respects. First, an architect needs a client, someone who is committed to paying for the end result and, second, the master architect will employ assistants who themselves may contribute much to the final structure of the building. This may have the effect of reducing the personal contribution of the commissioned architect unless the strength of his personality and his creative abilities are sufficient to leave their stamp on all aspects of the work. He is required to bring a recognizable personal quality/style even to apparently unimportant details; what may be called the 'brushstrokes' of architectural design, the decorative elements, the fittings, surface textures, colours and any other minor elements that contribute to the finished work. As we shall see, Wright had this requirement in abundance. He is, moreover, one of only a few architects who is an international household name. It is a measure of his fame and, as we shall see, his achievement, that this is so. Interestingly, it is also surprising that there should be so few of his fame and stature when we consider that architects have rather more effect on our physical lives than any painter, writer, or composer.

There is one further difference between architecture and the other arts which has already been noted, and it is one that is of particular importance in the consideration of our subject. Architecture is a necessary art. The creation of buildings begins with a social need for them, from homes and factories to temples and theatres. They are visible to all and indispensible in any civilized society. Furthermore, they provide long-term living evidence of the intrinsic nature and values of that society. We can discover more about the past from the study of architecture than from any other single factor.

The role of the architect in society is for these reasons of primary significance. Not only may the product of his creation profoundly affect our life through its ability to satisfy practical, functional needs but, through the character and quality of the design, it may condition our aesthetic responses to the visible world. Such a responsibility on the part of the architect is not always realized or accepted. To be fair, of course, other factors outside his or her control, such as vested interests or the demands of clients, may prevent him from realizing his design intention. But the greatest of architects have usually been able to impose their own creative vision on the works they produce.

Of all the architects of this century, and to some extent in the history of building, Wright is the pre-eminent individualist. Not only did he largely contribute to the period style of the first half of this century but he added a 'handwriting' that is so personal that for it to have been adopted by others would have been obvious plagiarism or, at the very least, evidence of creative aridity. Conversely, through his work, writings and lectures on the philosophy of architectural design he became an exemplary influence on those who were to come after him. So personal was his work, nevertheless, that he has been seen by many observers as a 'one-off maverick'.

One factor, unimportant in itself, has contributed significantly in creating the almost mythic status that has attached itself to Wright's reputation. His very long life of 93 years coincides in time with the coming to maturity of the United States and American society was in its youthful, energetic and formative stage as he grew up. He was born only two years after the end of the Civil War and the assassination of Abraham Lincoln. The emotional and physical wounds of the vicious internecine war had not then healed, neither had even a pragmatic unity been achieved. By the time of Wright's death in 1959, two great Wars, with their unprecedented loss of life (including the devastation of the atomic bomb on Hiroshima and Nagasaki) in which the United States had played a leading part, had changed social values and mores beyond recognition. A highly industrialized United States had by then achieved its present dominance on the world stage, General Eisenhower was President of the United States and Richard Nixon his Vice-President.

In the professional architectural scene from the early years of the century Wright was increasingly recognized as a creative leader in American architecture and, despite a number of early dramatic setbacks, emerged by the 1930s as a world architect – the only native American to have attained this status. His three most important contemporaries at this time, younger by more than a decade, were Europeans; Walter Gropius, born 1883 and Mies van der Rohe, born 1886 (both originating from Germany) and Le Corbusier, born 1887 in Switzerland. Following the rise of Hitler in the 1930s, Gropius and Mies had both settled, in 1937, in the United States; Gropius after a two-year period working in England and Mies after closing the Bauhaus in Berlin, of which he was its last Director, in 1933. Much of their more important later work as both architects and educationalists was therefore accomplished in America. Le Corbusier remained in Europe and completed only one building in the United States. Although Gropius and Mies spent the latter part of their careers in America and Mies made a considerable impact on architectural development there, it was Wright who carried the reputation of the 'indigenous' architects as well as attracting the affection and respect of the public in general and perhaps going some way to encourage national chauvinism. Despite the scandals of his early life, Wright eventually became a national icon, confirming the observation made by the British writer Malcolm Muggeridge that if you live long enough your past is forgiven.

Frank Lloyd Wright was born on 8 June 1867 at Richland Center in Wisconsin. His father, William Cary Wright, came from an English Nonconformist family which had emigrated to New England in the 17th century and was himself an itinerant Baptist minister with a passion for music, which he also taught. His mother, William's second wife, Anna Lloyd Jones, 15 years younger than her husband, was the daughter of Welsh immigrants and a dedicated schoolteacher. Both parents contributed greatly to the development of their son's character and interests. Wright was caught up in his father's passion for Bach and Beethoven, later recognizing how the order and structure of music had influenced his perception of architectural form. From his mother, and he was the first of her three children, Frank acquired a strong respect for learning and the value that he derived from the Froebel system of children's games, to which she introduced him, had a significant effect on his later architectural career.

He was encouraged to arrange the primary shapes of maple blocks and coloured papers on a linear grid into patterns and groupings which furthered his appreciation of massing and volume as well as stimulating his imagination. William and Anna were married in 1866 and Frank was born 10 months later. In 1877, after they had lived in Massachusetts for some time, the family moved back to Wisconsin's state capital, Madison. They were not far from Spring Green where the Lloyd Joneses, Anna's family lived and the children formed a strong attachment both for their grandparents and the Spring Green farm where they spent their holidays.

When Wright was 18 years old the first of a number of dramatic and distressing events occurred which were to affect the course of his life and career. His father divorced his mother and vanished from the scene. The full effect of this devastating event in an outwardly settled life was not felt for a number of years but it undoubtedly helped shape Wright's own attitude to the supposed permanence and stability of marriage. He was initially fortunate in that, following one of the occasional visits his Lloyd Jones uncle made to his mother, he came in contact with the practical side of designing architecture when his uncle commissioned an architect, J. Lyman Silsbee, to design a chapel for the Lloyd Jones's farming community in Spring Green valley. His mother had always hoped that he would become an architect and sought to encourage him by giving him John Ruskin's volumes *The Stones of Venice* and *The Seven Lamps of Architecture*. Ruskin was then the great mentor of Victorian society on all matters concerning art and architectural appreciation and these two works remained important in the development of Wright's own philosophy. Despite his mother's sadness at his departure and the disapproval of the rest of the family, who did not wish him to leave home, he decided to go to Chicago to become an apprentice architect. He had been attending classes in the local university's engineering department for more than three years and had received some formal training in draftsmanship – in fact the only such training he ever received. He showed considerable drawing ability even at that time and was taken on by Silsbee in Chicago.

In 1871 Chicago had been devastated by a great fire and there was still much architectural work available when Wright arrived to join Silsbee in 1887 at the age of 20. Silsbee was much in demand and had been practising in New York before moving to Chicago in the early 1880s. His designs in the Shingle Style, so known because wooden shingles were used to cover both roof and external walls, was the first architectural influence that Wright received. He was, however, distinctly disappointed in what he saw as otherwise uninspired and derivative design and left Silsbee's office to join the highly successful practice of Adler and Sullivan in 1888 on a five-year contract as a draftsman.

Adler and Sullivan were in the mainstream of architectural development in America from the time the partnership was formed in 1883 until 1895 when Adler left the firm. New York and Chicago were the two main centres for the development of skyscraper design and the World Columbian Exposition in Chicago in 1893 attracted wide attention. Sullivan provided a great arched doorway in Romanesque style for the exhibition and Wright contributed to the design.

In order to understand the position that Wright occupied in the development of the modern architectural scene it will be helpful first to look at what was happening in American and European architecture from the middle years of the 19th century when Wright was born.

During most of the second half of the 19th century an interesting architectural dispute, which has come to be known as the 'Battle of the Styles', provided architects and critics with a platform for dissension which was eventually to have a healthy effect on subsequent architectural thinking. The argument centred on what could or should be considered a correct style for a developing industrial society and, in particular, whether the medieval Christian, which might be regarded as the bedrock of the Western conscience or the Classical tradition, which traced its origins through the Renaissance back to the great civilizations of Greece and Rome and which formed the greatest part of Western architecture, was to continue to be the style for the future. Wright was born while what can, in retrospect, be seen to have been an arid artificial conflict was at its most intense. The Arts and Crafts Movement, well known through the writings and activities of William Morris and John Ruskin, participated in the debate on the side of medievalism in seeing the dignity of labour and the pursuit of good craftsmanship as characteristic of that age, concepts sadly lacking in an age of developing industrialization. That there could be a new and different non-historicist style that might be more valid and satisfying than either, did not readily occur to the disputants. But Wright's reading of Ruskin and his attachment to many of his beliefs concerning craftsmanship and ornamentation led him to be sympathetic to the Ruskinian philosophy.

By the turn of the century, not only had the affair become irrelevant but a new style, known as Art Nouveau, had emerged. Its development in America, in which the young Wright participated, contributed directly to the eventual evolution of his own highly personal aesthetic. Art Nouveau, as the name implies, was looking towards a new style which is seen in Europe in the work of such

architect/designers as Hector Guimard who designed the entrances to the Métro stations in Paris, Antoni Gaudí with his fantasies in Barcelona and Victor Horta's houses in Brussels. In America, where the style was somewhat different from the European version, the most important contributor was Louis Sullivan. His strong decorative sense, derived at least in part from Ruskin's belief in ornamentation, led to a rich form of decoration in a variety of materials from iron to terracotta, which proliferated over his buildings and became a highly visible feature of his architecture.

While the stylistic struggle was engaging architects, another important and influential factor was emerging with the increasing industrialization of the great nations as a result of technological advances. One of the most notable in its impact upon architecture was the introduction of the rail transport networks throughout Europe and North America and the resulting new architecture required for rail stations. Neither medieval nor classical styles seemed essentially or even reasonably appropriate (although, as can be seen in the London station façades of St. Pancras and Euston, it is possible that they were ill-advisedly chosen). The more appropriate solution seemed to lie with an engineered structure, providing a vault over the platforms and a façade that reflected this, as can be found adjacent to St. Pancras in the double-arched façade of King's Cross station, designed by Lewis Cubitt. The use of such materials as cast iron and later, steel, encountered in the vaults of the stations behind various façades, offered a new building material which engineers and architects were quick to exploit.

The range of new materials useful to building processes was enlarged towards the end of the 19th century by the development of cast concrete and, through the introduction of strengthening steel rods, reinforced concrete. This material had new and considerable possibilities. The outward forms of buildings were no longer confined to individual units of structure but could be built in any shapes that could contain poured concrete, which could curve and swoop in flowing and seemingly unsupportable ways. It could also, in conjunction with frames of steel, provide large structures without any interruption of the surface. The use of these materials (together with the availability of larger panels of glass which industry had also developed) was, starting before the First World War and achieving an apparently irresistible and permanent supremacy by the 1930s, a new style, devoid of historicism. A steel framed structural base was employed for larger buildings, sometimes with the use of cantilevered elements providing the possibility of curtain walling in glass or concrete panels and best expressed in rectangular forms. This has come to be identified as the 'White Box' style. So universal was the belief that this was the

architecture of the future that any architect failing to wholeheartedly support the thesis was regarded as reactionary. This became more widely known as the 'International Style' after an exhibition of that name was mounted at the Museum of Modern Art in New York in 1932 and the book by Philip Johnson and Henry-Russell Hitchcock that accompanied it. Both exhibition and book were devoted to establishing the new non-historicist style. It is curious to say the least that Wright was included in neither, particularly as Hitchcock had written the most important survey of Wright's work up to 1941, *In the Nature of Materials*.

The new technology and materials also inspired a new thinking about the forms that buildings could take using all available structural methods. Buckminster Fuller and the Keck brothers explored the use of steel, Fuller in the Dymaxion House (1927) and geodesic domes, and the Keck brothers in The House of Tomorrow and The Crystal House (both 1933). Although these experiments and others did not then succeed commercially they pointed the way to another building possibility which led in the 1970s to High Tech architecture such as the Pompidou Centre in Paris.

In the event, the apparently impregnable position of the White Box only lasted until the

OPPOSITE
Henry Hobson Richardson
(1836-86)
Trinity Church, Boston, Mass.
(1873-77)

Richardson's most widely publicized building stands at one end of Copley Square, facing, at the other end the Boston Public Library by McKim, Mead and White built in an Italian Renaissance palazzo form. The contrast between these two important examples of 19th-century architecture exemplifies the Battle of the Styles which was in progress during their construction. Richardson's church expresses his attachment to the Romanesque style with its round-headed arches and reflects his opinion that it reveals the best of both Roman and Gothic features. The importance of the Richardsonian influence on Wright can be seen in his use of the round arch in many of his early works, for example the *porte cochère* for his early Winslow House (1893).

Louis Sullivan (1856-1924)

INTRODUCTION

RIGHT
Louis H. Sullivan.
Carson, Pirie, Scott Department Store, Chicago, Ill.
1899-1904

Detail showing typical Sullivan Art Nouveau decoration on overhanging entrance canopy.

BELOW
Louis H. Sullivan.
Stock Exchange, Chicago, Ill. 1896

Main entrance. The heavy dominating Romanesque round-headed arch, continuing the Richardsonian influence, reveals the influence of Sullivan on Wright in, for instance, the Francisco Terrace apartments completed in the previous year (page 26).

1960s by which time Wright had already died. His view of this style during his lifetime was one of ambivalence. While he was enthusiastic in his exploration of the technology and materials newly available, at the same time he deplored the baldness of the forms and lack of interest in the surface treatment that seemed to him characteristic of the European architectural scene. His interest in decoration, the embellishment of surfaces, was part of the tradition he inherited from his mentors, and this in itself is revealing of his architectural philosophy.

To understand this, the architecture of the later 19th century in America requires some comment. The most influential figure in mid-19th-century American architecture was Henry Hobson Richardson whose career, cut short by over-indulgence, was crucial to the development of an identifiable American character. His masterpiece, the Marshall Field Wholesale Store, Chicago (1885-87), now destroyed, was clad in Romanesque-based stylistic elements which may still be seen in another of his buildings, Trinity Church in Boston (1873-77), perhaps his most characteristic surviving work. One frequent feature of Richardson's designs was a semi-circular, heavy neo-Romanesque arch. This was also later to be found in the work of the Chicago partnership of Adler and Sullivan, massively exemplified in the Columbian Exposition arch already mentioned. Through them, this feature is often encountered in Wright's own work. This arch and other decorative elements associated with the Romanesque style represented an essentially American aspect of the *fin de siècle* style associated with the Art Nouveau movement and reached its finest expression in the work of Adler and Sullivan, most specifically and importantly in the decorative designs of Sullivan.

As will be realized, the Adler and Sullivan partnership was seminal to Wright's career. He greatly revered Louis Sullivan, whom he called his *Lieber Meister* (Beloved Master), and it was while working for the firm that he designed his first buildings.

It was here that his architectural career really began. As already noted, his admiration for Sullivan was unbounded and, though largely unacknowledged, he also learned a great deal from Adler whose engineering passion contributed to Wright's rapid technological development. Wright did, however, believe that the dictum usually ascribed to Sullivan 'Form Follows Function' was in fact coined by Adler. Sullivan was recognized as the most important figure, with perhaps Louis Tiffany, in the development of Art Nouveau in America and Wright's attachment naturally followed, resulting in the strong decorative elements always apparent in his work.

Wright remained with Adler and Sullivan for nearly six years (1888-93) and while there was

married to Catherine Tobin. With Sullivan's help, through an advance in salary, he bought a plot of land at Oak Park, then a rural outskirt of Chicago, on which he built his home in the same year, 1889.

Adler and Sullivan were engaged on major architectural projects in and around Chicago and the unprofitable design of smaller houses was largely undertaken by junior architects' assistants in the office. Wright had by this time become the chief assistant and in 1890 was made responsible for the firm's domestic building. In this position he had the opportunity of taking on extra work which necessitated labouring late into the night at home. As demand expanded and his personal reputation increased, he undertook commissions on his own account – what he described as 'bootlegging'. At least part of the reason for this extra-curricular activity was the added expense of providing for his rapidly growing family – five children in the first nine years. These house commissions were mainly in his own locality around Oak Park and his early personal work can best be studied there. When Sullivan discovered what Wright was doing, he understandably felt badly betrayed by someone he had fully trusted. Wright left in 1893 (the start of a breach lasting 20 years), after which he set up his own practice and began his astonishing progress to fame.

In the period to 1900 Wright developed much of the design philosophy that conditioned and controlled his future work. By 1909 the first stage in his career was completed. This included what has come to be known as the 'Prairie Style'.

Wright, with other interested architects in the Chicago area who were concerned in creating a

continued on page 17

Frank Lloyd Wright's Own House and Studio, Oak Park, Chicago, Ill. (1889-1909)

The legacy of the Richardsonian Shingle Style of domestic architecture can be seen in this early work commenced soon after Wright joined Sullivan's office and had married Catherine Tobin. The rapid growth of his family necessitated extension and revision. Since, throughout his career, he liked to make alterations to finished designs where he believed improvements were possible, it is not surprising that the work eventually covered more than ten years. There are already evidences of individualist stylistic features such as the overhanging eaves and the separating terrace walling with entrance pylons and concrete flower urns. Internally, the open planning has already become a feature of his work. The fireplace in the main living area is formed from the ubiquitous half-circle arch. Extensions included a playroom with a barrel vault in 1893. The studio was added in 1898 and this included an octagonal library and a drafting workroom of two storeys with a suspended balcony. It was top-lighted, the first example of a feature of many of his later buildings and seen fully exploited in his Johnson Administration Building of 1936-1939.

Frank Lloyd Wright's Own House and Studio, Oak Park, Chicago, Ill. (1889-1909)

FAR LEFT
This illustration shows the relationship between the early house with steep pitched roof and the later studio on the right.

ABOVE
Detail of decorative columns with sculptures by Richard Bock.

LEFT
A decorative plaque stating Wright's name and profession.

RIGHT and OPPOSITE
Frank Lloyd Wright's Own House
and Studio, Oak Park, Chicago, Ill.
(1889-1909)

Ornamental urns at the entrance, an
early use of a decorative form much
employed by Wright in domestic
buildings and referred to by one client
as 'those flowerpots!'

continued from page 13

more ingenious and useful provision of space
through simplified construction and less
complicated decorative or stylistic detailing,
developed the Prairie Style, a name which
suggested the West – single-storey log cabins with
overhanging eaves and low pitched roofs. Wright
was the best known exponent of the style leading to
the impression that it was invented by him and
copied by others. While this is not so, it is
undoubtedly true that his exploration of spatial and
constructional possibilities in these early houses
had a profound effect on the design of all his
subsequent buildings, including large scale public
works such as the Larkin Administration Building
(1904). Wright listed nine principles which were to
be unified in the Prairie house design as follows:

   1. Number of parts to be minimized to
     produce a unity.

2. House to be integrated with site by emphatic
   horizontal planes.
3. Rooms as boxes to be replaced by spaces
   created through the use of screens and
   panels.
4. House to be raised on a platform above
   ground level with main living on upper floor
   to provide better all-round views.
5. Light screen windows to replace rectangular
   window holes in walls.
6. Materials minimized in number and with
   ornamentation expressive of each material
   and all designed for industrial production.
7. All services (plumbing, heating, lighting
   etc.) to be incorporated as architectural
   features into the building fabric.
8. Furnishing in keeping with building.
9. No 'fashionable decorators' to be employed.

William H. Winslow House, River Forest, Chicago, Ill. (1893)

Wright's first independent commission after leaving Sullivan was for his friend William Winslow. The house carries a number of features that became characteristic of his domestic designs, most notably, perhaps, the emphasis on the ground floor and the platform foundation that suggests the anchoring of the structure to the ground and provides a stylobate-type base. The first floor appears to float indeterminately over the ground floor and only to be held down by the heavy overhanging eaves. The façade is symmetrical and rectangularly centralized although Wright introduced a simplified Richardsonian arch for the *porte cochère*. The wide entrance is bounded by two large urns.

Internally, on the ground floor, there is a library as well as the usual living rooms while the first floor is devoted to bedrooms and services. An octagonal pavilion was originally intended to balance the *porte cochère* but this was never built.

The characteristics of these early houses are now familiar; a central service core incorporating ducted heating and open fires, multiple levels, platforms and structural screens guiding an internal spacial flow, while retaining a conscious feeling of unity in the whole. The unity of the buildings was emphasized by a low platform of concrete or stone which replaced the usual foundations and damp basement and offered a dividing line between land and structure. The use of decorative single, personally-designed elements, such as light fittings and furniture, added to the sense of total integration. Wright's overriding concern for the proper use and care of materials was another constant factor in all the buildings.

During the period to 1909, Wright completed a number of modest houses and five large luxurious dwellings as his practice expanded outside the Chicago area. One of the most ambitious and dramatic of these houses was the Darwin D. Martin house (1904) in Buffalo, New York. Other examples of his work of the time include the W. H. Winslow house (1893), in River Forest, Illinois, then a suburb of Chicago next to Oak Park, the first truly independent house to be completed after leaving Sullivan; the Chauncey Williams House, also at River Forest (1895) and reflecting a Richardsonian influence; his own studio in Oak

Park (1895) which was used by him, together with his home, as a source of design experiment so that several details of plans and structure came to be incorporated in later houses; the Joseph Husser House in Chicago (1899) incorporating the first cross-shaped plan and so hedged in by later building that the original amenities were lost and the house demolished; the Warren Hickox House (1900), the first Prairie house; the Ward W. Willitts House, Highland Park, Illinois (1902), on a cross plan and 'the first masterpiece among the Prairie houses' according to Hitchcock. Another of the more luxurious houses was the Avery Coonley House, Riverside, Illinois (1908) and in the same year the Isabel Roberts House in River Forest (1908), a fine Prairie house; and the Frederick C. Robie House (1909), in Chicago – widely regarded as the finest in the style which also incorporated new structural ideas.

The same period also saw the completion of two of Wright's most significant early public buildings, the Larkin Administration Building (1904), in Buffalo, New York, already mentioned, and the Unity Temple, Oak Park (1906). Each of these buildings, intended for very different uses, reveal his innately sensitive perception of the necessary character that should be an inherent part of the design. However, it has been suggested by

continued on page 34

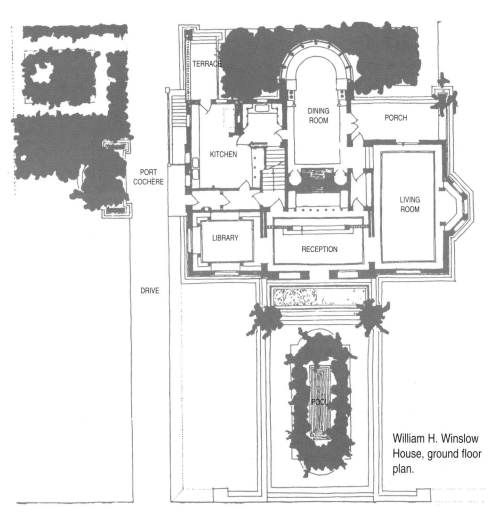

William H. Winslow House, ground floor plan.

Rear of William H. Winslow House showing tower and dining room bay providing strong contrast to flat symmetrical front elevation.

OPPOSITE
George Blossom House,
Chicago, Ill. (1892)

A unique example of the old Colonial classicism, found most typically in New England, in the executed work of the young Wright. There is an innate elegance and understanding of the academic demands as well as an interesting interpretation of the Serlian/Palladian window. The house

appears to stand on a podium surmounting a low stylobate. The porch, semi-circular in plan with exterior steps from the stylobate platform, is in a careful Ionic order. It is an indication that although Wright never used it again he had clearly understood what he was rejecting.

ABOVE
Walter Gale House, Oak Park,
Chicago, Ill. (1893)

This charming small scale house was, like the Blossom House, one of Wright's 'bootlegged houses', as he described them, since they were undertaken outside his working agreement with Sullivan while he was still employed by him and which led to his leaving the firm and setting up on

his own. The Gale House is one of three Wright built for Walter Gale in the same avenue in Oak Park. The one illustrated was for Gale himself while the other two were for speculation, though Walter's brother Thomas later bought one of them. They are not typical of Wright but do carry some elements developed by him in his Prairie houses, notably the excessive overhang of the eaves and the multi-angled corner rooms.

Nathan G. Moore House, Oak Park, Chicago, Ill. (1895)

The house as it now appears is much closer to the character of Wright's work in the 1920s than it is to the time that it was originally built since, after a fire in 1922 which nearly destroyed it, Wright redesigned its exterior. The original house was in the half-timbered Tudor style then very popular and only Wright's need for work persuaded him to undertake the commission. It says something for his singleness of direction that even though the house was much admired and brought him a number of requests for similar mansions, he did no more in the Tudor idiom.

Wright was asked to rebuild above the ground floor and the result reflects the Japanese influence of the recently completed Imperial Hotel in Tokyo. The squat urns and bulbous balustrade were survivors of the first design.

EARLY WORK 1889-1909

Chauncey I. Williams House, River Forest, Chicago Ill. (1895)

The first indications of a Japanese influence in Wright's work can be seen in this original design. Wright had been exposed to Japanese culture through the Columbian Exposition when he had worked on Sullivan's vast Romanesque decorative arch. In the Williams house the chimney stack, rising between two round-headed dormer windows, seems almost to have been inspired by a Samurai headdress. The overlapping of the eaves to a dominating extent, while providing a strong horizontal, also seems to add a note of mystery to the composition. Wright here introduces an idiosyncratic individualism which is possibly the first expression of his determination to follow his own direction without reference to his peers.

Francisco Terrace Apartments, Chicago, Ill. (1895). Demolished 1974

Wright was already beginning to get larger, more important commissions than the houses in and around Oak Park and his first multiple housing units appeared in 1895, the Francis Apartments and the low-cost, more interesting Francisco Terrace

apartments. The Francis Apartments are often considered Sullivanian but some of the features of Sullivan's work at this time, as Hitchcock has suggested, are more Wright than Sullivan. The Francisco Terrace flats are more dramatically composed, dominated by the terracotta-faced Romanesque archway with foliated spandrels, which led into a rectangular

courtyard onto which all the apartments, except those facing the street, opened. It was an innovation that Wright intended as a model for urban density living but the whole complex fell into neglect, disrepair and ultimately destructive vandalism and the buildings were demolished in 1974. However, the archway was re-erected in Oak Park in 1977.

Isidor Heller House, Chicago Ill. (1897)

The most interesting aspect of this house is the nature of the building site and the effectiveness of Wright's design. A very long thin rectangle restricted Wright's usual spatially-flowing design around a central core and the result was a most ingenious solution. The house was placed on one side of the lot with the outside wall running almost flatly around two-thirds of the total length of the plot. The other long side was broken and varied with flower beds and different levels, interrupted by steps. Internally, the principal rooms were placed crosswise and linked by a hall of the same long proportions as the building plot. The house is of three floors, the third smaller storey above the main roof covering the first floor being decorated with a frieze of nude female figures by Richard Bock. The house is built of a delicate grey and buff brickwork and the doorway is surmounted by a deep relief tripartite panel, flanked by stone columns. The usual broad heavy urns are included. This was altogether an unusual house for Wright.

Isidor Heller House, ground floor plan.

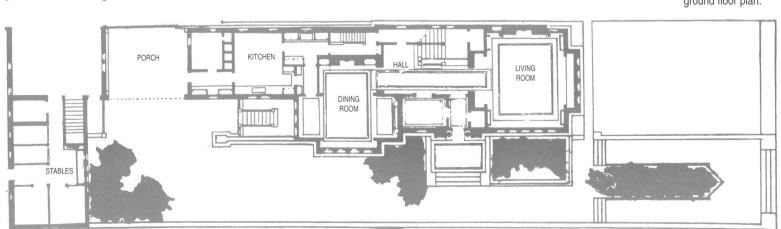

The influence of the designs Wright produced for the Curtis Publishing Company and published in the *Ladies' Home Journal* was greater than his actual architecture in earning him a national reputation. The difference in the designs from the usual Colonial Style, and the fact that they were supplied in the form of working drawings for five dollars each, disseminated and popularized the basic Prairie Style in which they were constructed. The idea was to demonstrate that an inexpensive house of individuality and personality could be built. The first design was costed at $7,000 and the second, described as a 'small house with lots of room in it' at $5,800. Other designs included a square concrete house and, in 1907, a fireproof plan. In basic character these designs were an expression of the Prairie Style. The illustration shows the main features; the low pitched roofs with wide overhanging eaves, the low platform defining the relationship with the ground (much as the three-stepped classical stylobate did for the Greek temple, such as the Parthenon), the spreading open internal ground plan and the non-historicist rural character. It will also be noted that the ubiquitous Romanesque doorway has been incorporated as well as the large squat garden urns.

**RIGHT
Warren Hickox House, Kankakee, Ill.
(1900)**

This small house is cruciform in plan with an extended living room completed at either end by a truncated octagon (a favourite form of Wright's) to create a music room at one end and the dining room at the other. The largely open asymmetrical plan includes kitchen and pantry on one side and the reception hall on the other. The upper floor contains four bedrooms and one bathroom.

BELOW
Arthur Heurtley House, Oak Park, Chicago, Ill. (1902)

The most notable innovation in this Prairie Style house near Wright's own house in Oak Park is the emphasis on the horizontal achieved by the simple addition of protruding brick courses. They also increase a rustic effect of board and batten through the brown Roman brick. The house is set on the usual low podium of concrete. The characteristic semi-circular entrance is fronted by a protecting wall which was originally surmounted by the usual large urns. The uncluttered lines and solid simplicity of the design is confirmed in the strong single roofline with the eaves overhang unifying the upper storey multiple-casement fenestration which Wright called a 'light screen'. Between the two piers on the lower floor is the playroom and the living room is located above. The house, square in plan, fronts the street with a very private aspect. It is one of the finest of Wright's early Prairie houses and Wright acknowledged later that the Japanese influence was already spreading to the exclusion of insignificant detail and attention to the natural beauty of materials.

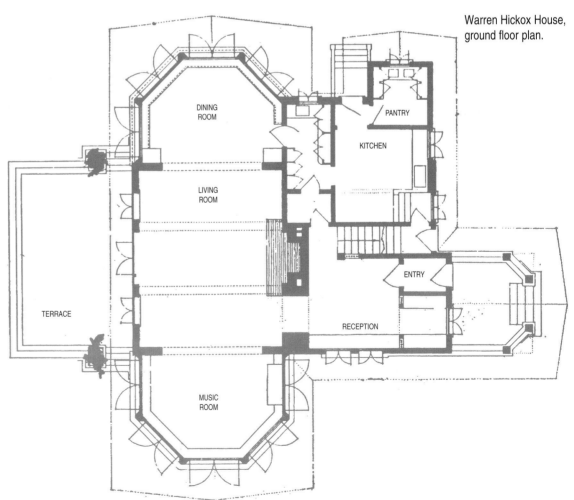

Warren Hickox House, ground floor plan.

DINING ROOM

PANTRY

KITCHEN

LIVING ROOM

TERRACE

ENTRY

RECEPTION

MUSIC ROOM

Ward W. Willitts House, Highland Park, Ill. (1902)

Henry-Russell Hitchcock describes this house as 'the first masterpiece among the Prairie houses' and both the elevation and the plans show an assurance and control in handling the cruciform shape and the combination of masses which spread from the central core. This is a large house with servants' quarters, including a butler's pantry on the ground floor as well as entry hall, living room, dining room and kitchen. The upper floor includes three bedrooms, library and nursery and is roofed by a clear cruciform construction while the ground floor roof extends to cover the dining room and porch on one side and the *porte cochère* on the other. A calm and unified dignity emanates from the house set on the usual concrete base which raises the living quarters above the spacious grounds. The structure is of steel and wood with plaster and exterior wood trim. The visual opposition of the light plaster and the dark wood trim is carefully controlled in the flat planes and vertical and horizontal dark linear trim.

The interior ground floor is a most effective expression of Wright's desire to provide a continual spatial flow and represents his personal response to the traditional boxes within a box design.

Example of glass panel decoration.

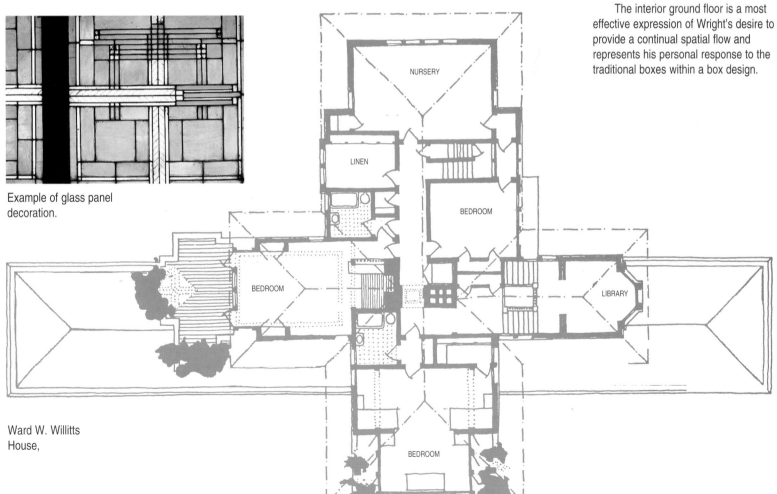

Ward W. Willitts House,

NURSERY

LINEN

BEDROOM

BEDROOM

LIBRARY

BEDROOM

William G. Fricke House, Oak Park, Ill. (1902)

Although this house includes many unusual features that are essentially Wrightian, a comparison with the Heurtley House of 1902 will indicate that it is more a rambling aggregate of related elements than a unified whole and looks more to detail than is characteristic of his work. It seems evident that Wright is determined to break the box mould with a stamp of individualist originality. The house is one of the tallest of the Oak Park houses and is on three floors, each of which is indicated with an emphatic roofline. A narrow entrance is surmounted by three tall windows, two of which run through a stairwell while the third rises through one floor into another. The street front also includes another feature which was becoming a characteristic of Wright's designs; a triangular window plan also repeated in the Heurtley House.

OPPOSITE BELOW and BELOW
Susan Lawrence Dana House, Springfield, Ill. (1903)

Wright was given an unusual commission by Susan Dana, a member of the Springfield élite. An unlimited budget and a design to surround an existing house, which Mrs. Dana found too small for the lavish entertaining she anticipated, resulted in a building large in scale, so large that it resembles a public building rather than a home. This feeling was emphasized in 1905 through the addition of a library by the side of the new house and reached by a raised, covered walkway. For the first time, Wright, with the freedom provided by unlimited resources, included two-storey rooms – the gallery, for the use of the local artistic community, the vaulted dining room with a sensitive monochromatic frieze by George Niedecken and the entrance hall.

One of the most significant detail elements of the house is the extensive use of decorative glass – mostly supplied by the Lindon Glass Company to Wright's designs – in fact, he designed more glass for this than any other building. Also included was sculpture by Richard Bock, one of Wright's favourite exponents of the form, and Wright designed most of the furniture and fittings. The house is cruciform in plan, with all the main rooms on the open ground floor and the bedrooms and offices on the upper floor.

continued from page 18

Brendan Gill in his biography of Wright that the source of inspiration for both buildings was the highly regarded Secession house in Vienna by Josef-Maria Olbrich. Nevertheless, the monumental frontage of the Larkin Building with its air of introspection and forbidding solidity personifies industrial strength and the mask of secrecy surrounding business practices. The brick and stone exterior suggests a formidably aggressive permanence but it was, in fact, bought by a wrecking firm in 1949 for a trivial price and torn down in the following year. By contrast the Unity Temple, constructed in poured concrete as a single mass on a smaller scale, is an invitingly domestic building with a richly decorated interior, revealing a sensitivity in the surface design which Wright carried through to all his work and which became a

recognizably personal element of his creative genius.

In 1904, with hindsight, the origin of a great change in Wright's life may be discerned which presaged both success and tragedy. Among his houses of 1904 was the Edwin H. Cheney House in Oak Park. Wright was immediately attracted to Cheney's wife, Mamah, although he was still married and the father of a large growing family. Mamah was a liberal-minded trained librarian, a lively and interesting person. Friends sensed the dangers inherent in their relationship and to distract Wright from a potentially disastrous infatuation suggested that Mr. and Mrs. Ward Willitts, who were also clients, should invite him to join them on their visit to Japan. Their accepted offer rekindled Wright's interest, fired by the Columbia Exposition, in all things Japanese. He became an avid long-term collector of Japanese prints and a certain Japanese influence began to manifest itself in his Prairie houses.

The trip was not successful, however, in deflecting Wright's interest in Mamah and in 1908 he asked Catherine, his wife, for a divorce. She requested that he wait for a year and although Edwin Cheney agreed to his wife's divorce, nothing was settled by the time that Wright departed for Berlin in the following year to oversee the publication of a prestigious portfolio of his work, planned by the established German publisher Ernst Wasmuth. It subsequently emerged that Mamah Cheney had joined him en route and that they had registered in a Berlin hotel as man and wife. The news, which quickly reached Oak Park, caused a public scandal in those less permissive days.

continued on page 48

The extraordinary and innovative qualities of this, the first of Wright's large scale commercial buildings, are of such interest that its destruction is nothing less than an architectural tragedy. That it cannot be fully illustrated in colour should not diminish appreciation of its importance.

The Larkin company was not a manufacturer but a mail order firm requiring a large and closely related secretarial and administrative staff and highly organized filing and storage areas. One of Wright's clients in Buffalo was William E. Martin and his brother, Darwin, joined the firm to replace one of the original founders. Wright was recommended as architect for the new administration building and his solution, although much criticized for its monolithic looks, was, he contended, a clear example of form being integrated to function – following his *Lieber Meister*'s precept.

The building is of brick and its frontage calls to mind something of the great Egyptian pylon-fronted temples. The sculptured globes by Richard Bock, while emphasizing the solidity of the otherwise undecorated brickwork, add an element of visual interest to the severe rectangular forms of the structure. Wright was much concerned to establish the integrated art and function elements of his work, claiming that buildings had the same right to be termed works of art as a locomotive, liner or battleship.

Internally, the whole of the core was an open space, lit from above like an *atrium* in which the secretarial and clerical staff worked while the senior staff and executives were located in the tiered galleries on either side. These were lit by the banked windows which were separated by piers running the length of the side wall in a way that implies a steel frame: suggestions have been made that Wright would have preferred this form of construction. A further important innovation was the introduction of air conditioning – its first commercial use. The clear, uncluttered appearance was achieved by the insetting of filing cabinets into the spaces between the piers. All the metal office furniture and fittings were designed by Wright.

35

Darwin D. Martin House, Buffalo, New York (1904)

The plan of the house that Wright built for David Martin while the Larkin Building was under construction indicates that it was a large and expansive design which included a number of related buildings. One of these was a small house for Martin's daughter and her husband, the Barton House, which is on a compact cruciform plan and often regarded as a finer, more subtle design than the larger house. Wright had already built a very successful house in Oak Park for William Martin, David's brother, without the constant dissension and bickering which accompanied the construction of this later house. Wright was, as usual, insistent on his intentions being carried out exactly with the result that costs and time overran.

The design was based on the *Ladies' Home Journal* design of 1901 but the site and generous budget allowed the building of a grander Prairie-Style mansion with finer materials than were envisaged for the magazine design. From the *porte cochère* on the left, to the very large porch on the right, the spaces interlock in a changing directional pattern around the central core of the living room fireplace and include a large reception hall, also used as a subsidiary living room, kitchen, dining room and library. The small concealed main entrance is off the reception hall. Forming the long arm of a Latin cross plan is a glazed, 100-ft (30.5-m) long pergola leading to the conservatory through which there is access to the garage. The first floor accommodated the bedrooms. The house was on the usual low concrete podium and the usual large, low urns were present. It is the general consensus that the house, although on a mansion scale and costing the enormous sum of $100,000 (almost unheard of at that time) is too large for its own good, that the vernacular Prairie Style is not really appropriate – a view with which Wright appears to have concurred. It may be appropriate here to note that Wright's furniture – notably his chairs – are as uncomfortable as they look. As he himself ruefully observed in his *An Autobiography*. 'I have been black and blue in some spot somewhere almost all my life from too intimate contact with my own furniture.'

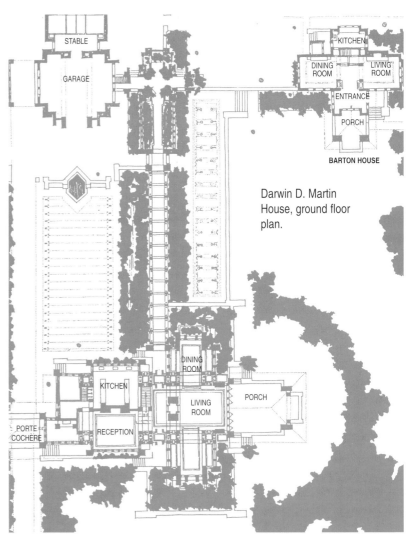

Darwin D. Martin House, ground floor plan.

ABOVE
Darwin D. Martin House, Interior.

LEFT
Edwin H. Cheney House, Oak Park, Chicago Ill. (1904)

The small single-storey house that Wright designed for Edwin and Mamah Borthwick Cheney is an unusual open plan with dining room, living room and library forming one continuous flowing space, the high pitched ceiling and the large windows accentuating a feeling of light and space. The fireplace alcove fronts the four bedrooms, dressing rooms and two bathrooms contrived within the limited space. The house is built of brick and is protected on the street side by a brick-walled terrace creating a sense of privacy and mystery, an attribute much favoured by Wright and encountered in a number of his houses. It may be recalled that it was during the construction of this house that Wright formed an attachment to Cheney's wife, Mamah.

EARLY WORK 1889-1909

Unity Temple, Oak Park, Chicago, Ill. (1906)

One of the major problems that face all older buildings is that the location in which they were originally built inevitably changes as time passes and it only the most powerful that can still dominate their surroundings. Unity Temple, because of its unique qualities, not only succeeds in this but still manages to express as much authority as it ever did. Of all the early public buildings that Wright designed, not excluding the Larkin Building, Unity Temple reveals more of the individuality and imagination of its creator. The Wright family were members of the Unitarian church community in Oak Park and when the neo-Gothic building was destroyed by fire in 1904, Wright was commissioned to build its replacement. The design was finished in 1905 but the building itself was not completed for some years.

With memories of the traditional church they had known still fresh in their minds, it is hardly surprising that the new building came as a considerable shock to the church authorities. It was like no other church

ABOVE Pier 'capitals'.

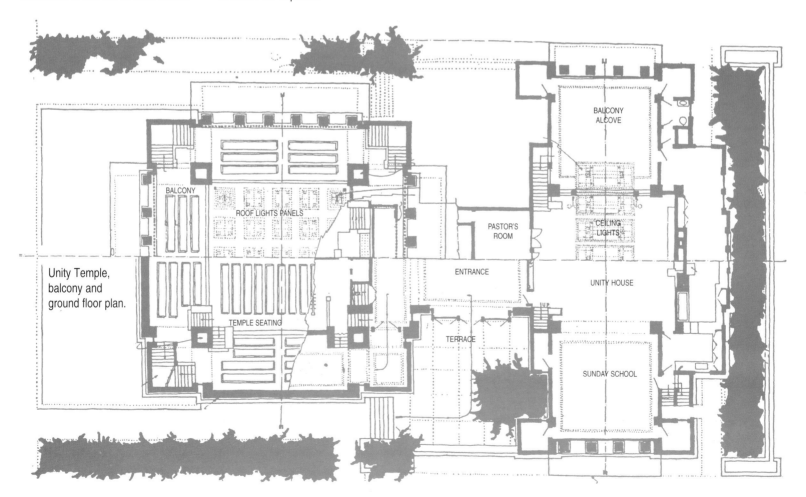

Unity Temple, balcony and ground floor plan.

BALCONY ALCOVE

BALCONY

ROOF LIGHTS PANELS

PASTOR'S ROOM

CEILING LIGHTS

ENTRANCE

UNITY HOUSE

TEMPLE SEATING

TERRACE

SUNDAY SCHOOL

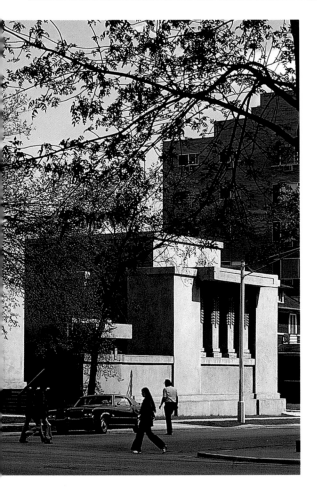

ABOVE Chair design for school house.

that they had ever seen, indeed, it is true to say that it was unlike any church that anyone had ever seen. It carried neither the familiar medieval or classical historicist elements and was, as Wright himself described it, 'a concrete monolith'. Wright had used poured concrete in limited quantities in some of his domestic buildings but this was the first use of the material in a public building after managing, on grounds of economy, to convince the building committee to use what most people even then regarded as an unattractive material. He also suggested that the effect of the small fine pebble aggregate, when washed clean, would come to resemble a rough granite. The whole building consisted of the chapel and a social hall which Wright called 'the good time place', and the entrance along the side of the building led, on the left to the social hall and on the right to the chapel. Wright saw the building as a temple and it has the forthright character of such early structures emphasized by the large piers at each corner possessing Egyptian overtones.

The interior is, however, perhaps of greater interest. The quality of calm intimacy and a sense of spiritual peace is all-pervading; it feels that it could not be other than it is – a place of worship. The effect of the roof lighting and the high side windows is restful and the soft colours and common identity of the whole decorative interior justifies the name Unity Temple.

Glass ceiling panel.

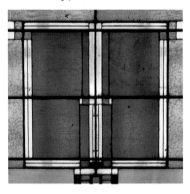

Frederick C. Robie House, Chicago, Ill. (1906-10)

There is a general consensus that the Robie House is one of the finest houses of Wright's early creative Prairie Style. It has many innovative features, some initiated by Robie himself during construction. Robie was a successful inventor and a manufacturer of automobile supplies and he asked Wright to design a modern house using as much new technology as seeemed to him appropriate. The result was closer in general plan to the early Heller House and on a similarly restricted site to the usual cruciform Prairie house plan but much more assured and adventurous. The narrow corner lot demanded a strong directional axis and Wright emphasized this with a long cantilevered roof of steel girders stretching over 20ft (6m) beyond the end of the wall supports. The house was of brick and concrete and the long horizontal lines, the large chimney rectangular at right angles to the length, and the prow-like diamond-shaped bays at either end so much suggest a great ship that local Germans dubbed it the *Dampfer* (steamship).

It is however the interior which is most innovative. The low ground floor, visually minimized by the terrace walling of brick with a concrete top course emphasizing the horizontal, includes a children's playroom, billiard room, concealed entrance hall invisible from the street, boiler room, laundry, integral garages and walled court. The living room, dining room, guest room, kitchen and servants' quarters are on the first floor with the master suite on the second partial storey. The revolutionary element is that the ground- and first-floor main areas are unwalled so that a continuous flowing openness is only partially interrupted by the large chimney stack. Wright also designed all the fixtures and fittings which, unusually, have all been retained and make the interior of exceptional interest. The house incorporates an additional number of inventive ideas contributed by Robie, such as an integrated industrial vacuum-cleaning system.

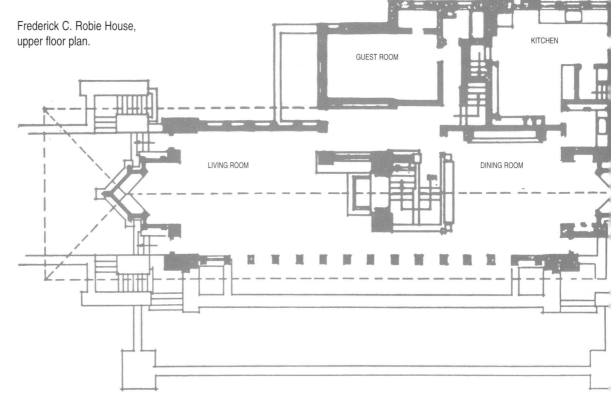

Frederick C. Robie House, upper floor plan.

GUEST ROOM

KITCHEN

LIVING ROOM

DINING ROOM

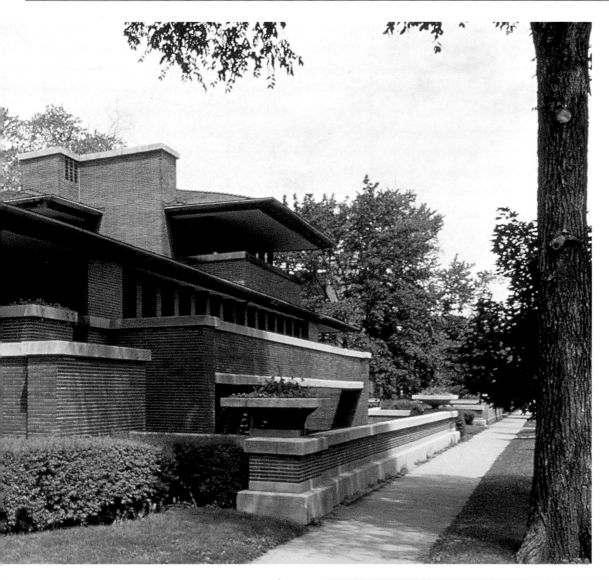

A slant-back chair, designed for the Robie House.

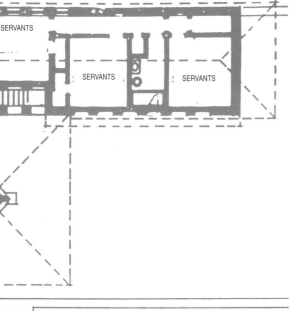

SERVANTS

SERVANTS

SERVANTS

View of the living room.

ABOVE Detail of the interior of the Coonley House.

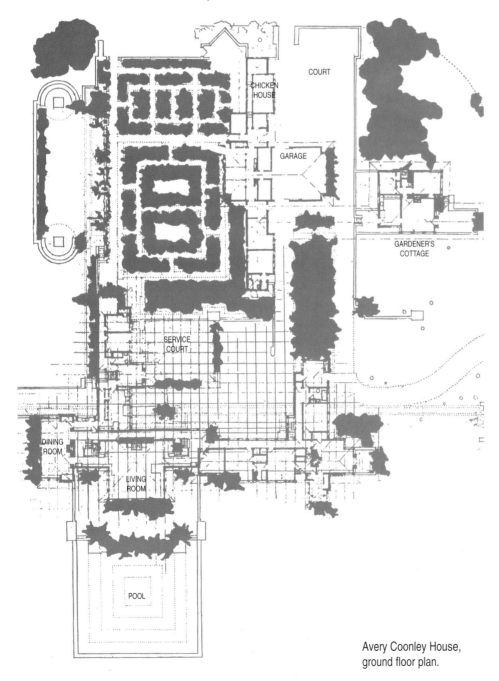

Avery Coonley House,
ground floor plan.

Avery Coonley House, Riverside, Ill. (1908)

Avery Coonley was not only an exceptional client but also a close friend. He gave Wright a generous budget, a virtual free hand and a large plot in the delighful surroundings of a well laid out community design by Frederick Law Olmsted, who with his partner, the English architect Calvert Vaux, was one of the most successful landscape architects of his time. Like the Heurtley and Robie houses the living areas are on the first floor, on this occasion at least, partly to minimize the effect of the level ground across which the house faced. On its large site the house is expansive in design and Wright's plan includes a pool, sunken garden, stable and garage block, gardener's cottage and what is described as a chicken house. The main house, to which was later added a Playhouse (1912), forms an L-plan with the servants' quarters making up the short leg. The large living room has a sloping glass ceiling providing overhead lighting and faces onto the pool terrace which offers a large private area for the family. One unique feature of the house is the banded decorative frieze in coloured tiling stretching along the upper storey.

RIGHT and INSET
Isabel Roberts House, River Forest, Ill. (1908)

The exceptional aspect of this small house is the extension of the ground floor living room into the upper floor. Although Wright had proposed such a feature as early as the first *Ladies' Home Journal* project, and had included it in such large projects as the Dana house, this was the first time that it had been ventured in a small house and does lend a sense of spaciousness to what is essentially a modest building. This is also helped by the continuous space flow from the dining through the living areas to the large porch. Three bedrooms and a servant's room are located on the upper floor.

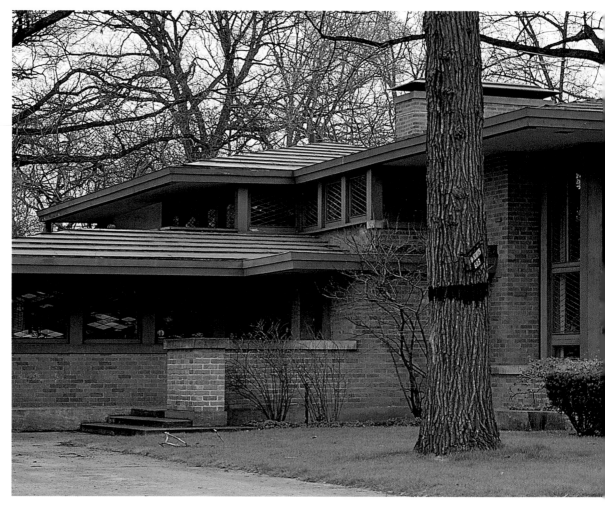

RIGHT
Mrs. Thomas H. Gale House, Oak Park, Ill. (1909)

Another house based on the first *Ladies' Home Journal* project with the added feature of a cantilevered balcony and a slightly elevated terrace. The living room also rises into the upper floor as in the Roberts house but without the open plan.

BELOW LEFT
Meyer May House, Grand Rapids, Mich. (1909)

In this house Wright had another opportunity to carry out his design with full freedom and the result is an attractive, friendly house with a number of original features characteristic of Wright's still-developing style. There are usually new external features to distinguish each design and in the May house a copper-sheathed lattice screen fronts the lower windows and the first floor, while pale brick walls with emphatic horizontal courses provide an interesting balance to their strong dark forms. Internally, Wright designed all the furniture and fittings and, of course, the decorative glass in the windows. The entrance hall is decorated with a mural of schematized hollyhocks by George Niedecken, somewhat reminiscent of William Morris's wallpaper style. Niedecken spent time in Europe and worked with the great Art Nouveau Czech designer, Alphonse Mucha, before he returned to America and founded a firm of interior architects and completed a number of works for Wright.

The May house was one of the last of the early stage of his career just before he went to Berlin to prepare the Wasmuth portfolios.

TOP
Lexington Terrace, Chicago, Ill. (1909)
Project design only.

Lexington Terrace was a scheme first envisaged in 1901 and resurrected in 1909 with somewhat modified elevations. Although the buildings were never erected the project does constitute a reminder of the large scale work that Wright was designing coterminously with the Prairie houses.

The design for Lexington Terrace was included in the Wasmuth portfolios. It is another housing development like the earlier-built Francisco Terrace, but on a much larger scale. The apartments were in two separate blocks with a central court around which two sets of apartments were placed back to back and with an open passageway between.

ABOVE
Edward H. Doheny Ranch Development, near Los Angeles, Calif. (1921)

This vast project would have been, to judge from the drawings made of the whole scheme (illustrated here) and the designs for individual buildings, not only the largest but also the most romantically unlikely of all Wright's imaginative fantasies. Even in the expansive years before the Wall

Street crash and the Depression it seems a project too far, destined, like the San Marcos-in-the-Desert and Lake Tahoe projects of the same time, never to be realized. The scale and grandeur of the Doheny Ranch does however emphasize, yet again, that Wright yearned for large scale architectural expression and was prepared to devote enormous creative energy to achieve it.

TOP
Sherman M. Booth House, Glencoe, Ill. (1911)

The Booth house was not erected until 1915 and was much less notable and interesting than the plans originally prepared in 1911 suggested. The illustration, prepared from the original plans, was made by Marion Mahony who worked in Wright's office, made many of his perspective renderings, completed some of his designs while

he was in Berlin and, in the year of this drawing married Walter Griffin who also worked for Wright. The quality of her visualizations made a significant contribution to the calibre of the work emerging from Wright's office.

ABOVE
San Marcos-in-the-Desert, near Chandler, Ariz. (1927)

This extensive project, not as grandiose as the Doheny Ranch scheme, was nevertheless also destined to fail, on this occasion directly through the arrival of the Depression. It was commissioned by Dr. Alexander Chandler and was to consist of a hotel and several houses built with textile blocks and intended

by Wright to demonstrate the versatility of the low-cost system. The decoration of the blocks, of which full-scale samples were made, consisted of a raised zigzag pattern abstracted from a cactus form. It is a matter of regret that this very complete and well conceived project should have remained unrealized since it most likely would have inspired other developments of equal importance.

FROM TALIESIN I TO TALIESIN III 1911-1925

continued from page 35

Taliesin I, Spring Green, Wis. (1911)

After the scandal his affair with Mamah Borthwick Cheney caused in Oak Park, Wright moved to the house he built on the hillside land that his mother had purchased near her relatives and within sight of the Hillside Home School he had built for his aunts in 1902. Taliesin became for Wright the centre of his life and work, expanding over the years and, as a result of the disastrous fires of 1914 and 1925, being subjected to almost continuous redesigns and modifications. It was a house, a studio, a farm and eventually incorporated the Hillside Home School. Taliesin became one of the best known houses in America and the centre of pilgrimage for all interested in the development of American architecture. The house reveals all Wright's preoccupations, particularly his interest in oriental styles. It was in the original house that the murder of Mamah and her children occurred soon after it was built.

Despite the damage done to Wright's moral reputation and, of course, to his architectural practice, the Wasmuth publications enhanced his international reputation and through the success of the published portfolios he acquired an influence in Europe, (including Britain) through his friendship, from 1900, with C. R. Ashbee, a well known designer and architect four years his senior. Two portfolios were issued, to the second of which Ashbee contributed an introduction. Wright was close to becoming an international architect at the age of 40.

On his return to America in 1911, still with Mamah Cheney, his position became increasingly difficult. In those proscriptive pre-war years his provocatively unconventional stance, and the continued refusal of Catherine to give him a divorce, resulted in a serious decline in his practice, although the Avery Coonleys continued to employ him as their architect and his mother provided him with the opportunity of building a splendid home, studio and farm on land she owned at Spring Green, Wisconsin. On its completion, the unconventional family moved in, the now-divorced Mamah (Borthwick), the still-married Wright and his mother. The other members of his mother's family, the Lloyd Joneses, were aghast and the new house, called Taliesin, became notorious. The name Taliesin, chosen by Wright, was that of a Welsh bard and seer (the name in Welsh means 'shining brow') and identified both Wright's Welsh origins and the vein of romantic mysticism that ran through his nature.

In these difficult times it is characteristic of Wright that, instead of adopting a contrite, modest and retiring attitude he actually managed to raise his public and professional profile through the design of his first skyscraper, the Press Building, (half as tall again as any then standing), for a real estate company in San Francisco. In the form of a thin slab with an overhanging slab roof, similar to that used in the Unity Temple, the design avoided the usual period additions and was in a form widely used later on. For its time, 1912, it was a remarkably prophetic design and shows something of the courage and tenacity that stood Wright in good stead throughout his life.

Wright's interest in Japanese prints kept his Far Eastern interests alive and it was fortuitous for him at that time that Japanese businessmen, including members of the Japanese Imperial household, were looking for an architect to design a hotel for visiting dignitaries. Wright's name came up, he was investigated, invited to Tokyo in 1913 and, having arrived there with Mamah, managed to secure the commission.

Although Wright had by now achieved an international reputation, the notion of a world architect hardly existed in those pre-war years. But Tokyo's Imperial Hotel, when built, established

Wright's world status. The hotel was completed in 1922 and in the following year the great Tokyo earthquake, which devastated the whole of the city, left the hotel virtually undamaged. Wright's reputation as an architect was thus firmly established but of more significance to him (and he was not a man greatly given to self-doubt) was the structural success of his original design.

The Imperial Hotel was a very large scale construction and while it was being built Wright was also engaged on another large project in Chicago known as Midway Gardens (1914). This was a complex of restaurants, clubrooms, bars and included an extensive uncovered central court incorporating a large bandstand. When built it was intended that it should become an important feature of south Chicago social life, but it did not catch on. The onset of Prohibition in 1919 seriously damaged its *raison d'être* and the whole complex was demolished in the 1920s.

In August 1914, as his career was beginning to flourish, tragedy struck. Wright was called to Taliesin where a serious fire had broken out. On the way he was joined by Edwin Cheney who had come to see his children who were living with Mamah, their mother. When they arrived, not only were they confronted with a devastating fire but, more horrifying, they found that Mamah, the two children (a boy and a girl) and four of Wright's employees had been murdered – hacked to death with an axe – by a demented house servant who had previously set the fire which had already destroyed two-thirds of Taliesin. Wright himself was devastated; only slowly and through devotion

Press Building, San Francisco, Calif. (1912)
Project. Model of Tower Block.

The most interesting aspect of this project is, perhaps, its date. The design for a concrete skyscraper with a simple slab form, integrated abstract vertical piers and broken horizontal window apertures is unlike any other contemporary work and an essentially individualistic Wrightian solution. The slotted slab overhang roof is an echo of the Playhouse roof of the same year. It is also yet another reminder of the diversified design programme on which Wright was engaged.

Avery Coonley Playhouse, Riverside, Ill. (1912)

The Playhouse was constructed in the grounds of the earlier Coonley house (1908) on a basic Greek cross plan. Its main internal feature is the stage, placed in one of the arms with dressing rooms to the rear. The central area was open with a kitchen in one arm and a workshop facing. Externally, the building is an exceptionally controlled massing of simple undecorated forms balancing horizontal and vertical in a design which Wright himself believed to be one of his most perfect creations.

Midway Gardens, Chicago, Ill. (1914)

Edward C. Waller Jr., the son of a friend and client of Wright's, conceived the idea of a grand pleasure complex in the heart of Chicago which would become the entertainments mecca for the city. It would consist of a large restaurant facing the street behind which a great open court with bandstand and stages would provide the equivalent of a beer garden or a modern version of London's Vauxhall Gardens. Wright agreed and the result was a combination of many of Wright's ideas up to that time.

It had everything except good timing. The first war started soon after its opening and, more specifically disastrous, Prohibition arrived in 1919. In addition, the building work did not progress at all happily although Wright completed the design very quickly – in days rather than weeks. The budget was $350,000 and only a part of this was raised before work started and throughout the building process cash was always in short supply. A number of artists were employed and displays of 'artistic temperament' caused tensions, a sculptor, Iannelli, failing to satisfy Wright's exacting standards. Henry-Russell Hitchcock in his book *In the Nature of Materials*, suggests that Wright was independently approaching the European artistic movements of the pre-war years, notably Cubism, and Iannelli's work was not up to the abstraction of forms that Wright was developing in painting and sculpture at the time.

The original plans reflected a distinctly cultural intention (Pavlova danced at Midway Gardens) for which the Chicagoans may have been intellectually unprepared. There was little knowledge of the European scene and the Armory Show in New York of the same year was the first exhibition in America to include modern European paintings and sculptures.

Eventually, after two years of losses, the whole complex was sold to a brewer who turned it into a German-type beer garden just in time to have it closed by Prohibition. It was demolished as a failure in the early 1920s, but photographs and drawings show what a splendid and uniquely inventive pleasure centre it might have been.

to work did he slowly recover.

Among the many who came to condole and console was a woman unknown to Wright who was destined to cause him untold aggravation and distress for a number of years. On a visit to Tokyo to supervise work on the hotel she accompanied him – not at his instigation – and he was unable to avoid her attentions which became increasingly unbalanced and vindictive. Nevertheless, Wright showed a strange reluctance to rebuff her totally – indeed he appeared to feel responsible for her behaviour, to the extent that when his wife, Catherine, finally divorced him to marry someone else, he actually married her. Her name was Miriam Noel, she was a sculptress, and soon after the marriage she too left him for another man but continued to pursue him with threats and lawsuits, severely disrupting Wright's attempts to advance his career.

Wright had not yet completed his work on the Imperial Hotel and during the First World War he continued to make long visits to Japan, usually from California. On one of his return trips in

California he met Aline Barnsdall whom he had known in Chicago. She was a patron of music and the theatre, particularly of the 'little theatre' movement. She had recently bought a hill in Hollywood and was keen to build a complex to include not only an experimental theatre but studios, shops and living accommodation. In addition, on the crest of the hill, she required a magnificent house in which to entertain and occasionally to live. Wright was commissioned and although he was mostly in Japan and had to delegate much of the work to an assistant, R. M. Schindler, who had studied Wright's Wasmuth portfolios in Vienna and had become attracted to America where he settled in 1914. The Barnsdall House, more familiarly known as the Hollyhock House (1920) because of the abstracted hollyhock-based decoration he extensively employed, was one of the finest of Wright's earlier buildings and Schindler himself subsequently became a highly respected and successful architect. Eventually the Hollyhock House became a community arts centre.

Back in the United States after the completion

FROM TALIESIN I TO TALIESIN III 1911-1925

**Imperial Hotel, Tokyo, Japan
(1914-1922)**

This was one of Wright's most important commissions in the second stage of his professional career and achieved such acclaim that Wright made his mark as an architect of world-wide celebrity and status. The very large complex forms an H-plan with the elaborate public areas on the crossing bar and the private bedrooms along the side arms. The supervision of the work necessitated Wright's presence in Tokyo for long periods during the First World War and in 1916 he settled there with his then companion, Miriam Noel, making occasional visits to America, usually California, during which he managed to keep his practice alive. The building of the hotel was not completed until 1922.

One of the major problems that confronted Wright was the frequency of earthquakes in the Tokyo region, a problem compounded by the great size of the site and the fact that the subsoil consisted of over 50ft (15m) in depth of mud. Wright's successful

solution, which he described as similar to the balancing of a tray on a waiter's fingers, consisted of grouped tapering concrete supports, driven into the subsoil with continuous concrete floors above floated on a varying height base. The second floor carried cantilevered rooms. The effectiveness of the engineering design solution was proved by the fact that soon after the hotel was finished a great earthquake destroyed most of Tokyo leaving the hotel nearly intact. Another factor, often unrecognized, was that Wright had included a number of pools in the court which, although treated decoratively, were primarily meant to be used in case of fire, and they proved invaluable as fire raged around the site. An important feature was that the walls of brick and concrete tapered as they rose upward to reduce weight and lower the centre of gravity.

The design of the details, both internally and externally, was ornate with Japanese and pre-Columbian overtones. The rough-surfaced lava stone used was carved into abstract geometric forms which provided a foil to the delicate brickwork.

Although demolished in 1968, an example of commercial cupidity and architectural vandalism, it is possible to get some notion of the quality and character of this uniquely important structure since the hotel entrance and the ornamental pool which fronted it have been reconstructed at Nagoya about 150 miles (240km) from Tokyo.

Aline Barnsdall House, 'Hollyhock House', Los Angeles, Calif. (1920)

Aline Barnsdall was an oil heiress, an actress and a rich patroness of the arts who knew exactly what she wanted and how this might be achieved – not Wright's ideal client – and tensions soon began to develop. However, since Wright was then a virtual expatriot in Japan, engaged with the building of the Imperial Hotel and paying only infrequent visits to California, the work proceeded largely without him, overseen by his assistant, R. M. Schindler.

The design of the house was completed by the end of 1917 and its relationship to the Imperial Hotel is evident. We have already noted that the decorative elements in the hotel design contain pre-Columbian influences and this is even more apparent in the Hollyhock House, with its solid block forms and its slightly battered superstructure, evoking the heavy lowering aspect of a Mayan temple. The dominant decorative motif is, of course, the hollyhock, from which Wright has succeeded in devising a rich modern version of the harsh Meso-American decorative style.

The magnificence of the hilltop site, with the mountain range behind the house to the north, emphasizes the great mass of the buildings from which all references to the Prairie Style have been removed. The plan reveals a centralized asymmetrical design in which all the activity areas are separate, as perhaps is appropriate in an artistic community. It might indeed be observed that the finished building has such a tight, private and enclosed aspect that it seems in direct opposition to the use an outgoing, liberal-minded client might have envisaged for it.

The Hollyhock house was only the second commission in California but it began a short series of houses that Wright designed there in the 1920s.

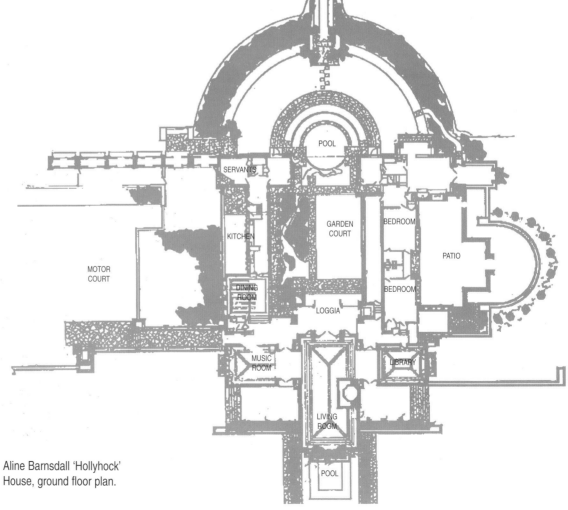

Aline Barnsdall 'Hollyhock' House, ground floor plan.

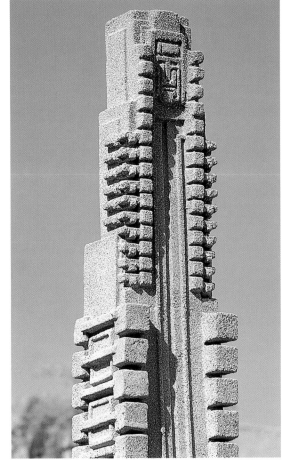

of the Imperial Hotel Wright, with typical creative energy and alert as always to the possible combination of art and structure, devised a process of building using unskilled labour and cheap materials. He decided to replace the much maligned and unattractive precast concrete blocks with a new form consisting of small precast concrete shells held together by steel rods to form double walls in a combination he called 'knitblock'. Since these shells could be formed to provide either plain or decorative surfaces, giving an overall ornate surface or grouped decorative elements, it was an extremely flexible way of enhancing the visual character of walling. He called it his 'textile block' system because of the steel rod warp and weft holding the structure together. Using this system Wright built a number of houses in California, the most notable being the Mrs. George Madison Millard House 'La Miniatura'(1923) in Pasadena, Alice Millard being the wife of a former client and a dealer in antiques. In addition, there was a house for Dr. John Storer (1924) on a hillside overlooking Los Angeles; and the even larger Charles Ennis House (1924). For another of his house designs, and ever sensible to the need for an aesthetic solution, Wright devised a form of corner window which avoided a corner post, allowing a wide angle of viewing from within a rectangular room space. With variations, he later frequently used this device for visual effect. He

also experimented, in the Samuel Freeman House, also of 1924, with concrete blocks inset with glass.

Wright's mother, who had always been close to him, died in 1923 and early the following year Louis Sullivan, who after a 20-year estrangement had become reconciled with Wright, also died in obscurity and near poverty: Wright was in Sullivan's house on the day that he died. The deaths of two people for whom he had great affection and who had been of primary importance to his early career, caused him great pain and sadness. His life up to then had been a strange and dramatic mixture of tragedy, success and happiness. It seemed set to continue that way when, a little later in the same year, he met a young and very talented lady from Montenegro, recently divorced and to whom he was immediately attracted. Olga Lazovich, known as Olgivanna, reciprocated; but it should be remembered that Wright was still married to Miriam Noel. It was not until four years later, in 1928, when he was eventually divorced, that he was free to marry Olgivanna with whom he remained for the rest of his life.

Wright continued to investigate and consider various structural possibilities. One major project of 1924, never realized but highly significant, was a skyscraper for the National Life Insurance Company in Chicago for which a method of construction was envisaged, later to be widely used by, and more usually associated with, Mies van der

OPPOSITE
Aline Barnsdall House, 'Hollyhock House', Los Angeles, Calif. (1920)
ABOVE
From the pool into the garden court.
BELOW
Detail of hollyhock decoration.

LEFT
Mrs. George Madison Millard House, 'La Miniatura', Pasadena, Calif. (1923)

The first house to be designed using the 'textile block' system (page 55), La Miniatura, is, as its name implies, a small house but built on three floors and, unusually, at the bottom of a ravine. Mrs. Millard had previously lived in a house designed by Wright and when he suggested his new system she was happy to entrust the project to him. The result was what has been described as a small architectural gem dropped into a magical forest. The overall use of the moulded blocks can be seen both internally and externally. Perhaps the most unusual feature, however, was that the furniture and fittings were not designed by Wright and the interior has always looked somewhat incongruous as a result. Mrs Millard was a dealer in antique furniture who operated from the house; the objects housed within were thus constantly being changed or rearranged.

Mrs. Millard was delighted with the house as was Wright himself who claimed in his autobiography that he would rather have built it than St. Peter's in Rome.

Rohe. The design took the form of a cantilevered steel or reinforced concrete frame clad with curtain walls, hung or supported on the cantilevered floors, which would provide more light internally and reduce the sense of massivity of the whole structure. Mies was thinking along the same lines at the time and although Wright's skyscraper was not as elegant or advanced as Mies's proposals, it is important to note that Wright designed or planned large scale buildings using new techniques through most of his working life. He was not, therefore,

solely concerned with the domestic buildings which had earned him his reputation. His National Life Building would have risen to 27 floors above ground, with three below, and would have consisted of a rectangular slab form with four transverse oriel-type bays. The whole was to be covered in sheeted glass and copper and it was intended that the interior space would be divided with movable partitions.

This constructive and socially advanced thinking on a large scale has rarely been

continued on page 66

National Life Insurance Company, Chicago, Ill. (1924) Project.

This perspective drawing indicates not only Wright's ability to coordinate the various elements of a multi-level structure but also to create a great unified building incorporating many of his decorative elements in a skyscraper, the almost invariable feature of which at this time was an historicist cladding style. The competition for the *Chicago Tribune* Tower in 1922 resulted in a late medieval design for what is essentially a modern industry, newspaper publishing. The *Chicago Tribune* Tower was completed in the year of Wright's National Life project and a comparison of the two buildings establishes that Wright's design aesthetic was very close to the advanced views then prevalent in Europe. In fact, Walter Gropius submitted a design for the competition which has affinities with Wright's National Life design.

OPPOSITE
Studio portrait, c.1940, of Frank Lloyd Wright with his wife Olgivanna.

Dr. John Storer House, Los Angeles, Calif. (1923)

Built on a hill site on Hollywood Boulevard, the Storer house was an incongruous structure to have appeared in the developing film city of the early 1920s and it remains so since it was one of the only four textile block houses that Wright constructed in Los Angeles. The sloping site demanded retaining walls on which a terrace was constructed for the two-storey house. The variety of levels within the house provide a sense of flow with which the actual building does not accord. At the centre is the living room with high fenestration on either side, the four bedrooms being contained on two floors at one end while at the other a small kitchen and a servant's room complete the accommodation. The Storer house is not one of Wright's majestic houses but Hitchcock calls it an 'elegant pavilion' and Wright described it as a little palace, like a Venetian palazzo. At one time the house was in a slow progress of decay, being covered with luxuriant Californian foliage; but it has been carefully restored, now providing a good example of Wright's use of his textile block system.

Charles Ennis House, Los Angeles, Calif. (1923-24)

This is the largest of the textile block houses and, as with the Hollyhock House, has the massivity of a great Mayan temple on its elevated, fully-terraced site and with full-length retaining walls. Although an integrated interlock system, here the pressure demands on the walls have resulted in bulging and cracking, unresponsive to all attempts to restore them. In the Storer house there is a balance between the areas of plain and decorated blocks but in the Ennis house there is such a proliferation of decoration that the essentially modern design, echoing coincidentally what was happening concurrently in Europe, is not immediately evident. Wright was rarely at the site and left much to his son Lloyd, a qualified architect, when dissensions arose. As a result, it has never been what might be described a happy house and the Ennises finally completed the work without Wright's agreement.

Taliesin III, Spring Green, Wis. (1925-59)

Wright's original house at Spring Green, Taliesin I, was a constant source of experiment in terms of design and building which he carried out for the rest of his life, elements of which he incorporated in many of his later structures. After the second Taliesin fire in 1925 the damage was so extensive that the smaller original structure was exchanged for a constantly expanding complex of buildings. The long first design, with building stops at each end, was enlarged in all directions and included a central large studio and gallery, separate quarters for Mr. and Mrs. Wright, a music room with stage, a hill garden and large chicken pens. Even after he had constructed his last Taliesin in the desert near Scottsdale, Arizona, Taliesin III continued to be his home.

OPPOSITE ABOVE
View of balcony with typical overhang roof.

OPPOSITE BELOW LEFT
Interior of living room with furniture, including carpet, designed by Wright.

OPPOSITE BELOW RIGHT
Detail of dining area.

Richard Lloyd Jones House, Tulsa, Okla. (1929)

The great fortress-like block house that Wright designed for his cousin, a successful newspaper owner in Tulsa, was different from the decorated blocks used in the Californian houses, since the blocks were large and undecorated, giving the house the forbidding appearance of a penitentiary. The exterior is also of a unique construction of closely spaced vertical piers from ground to roofline, the spaces in between being filled with windows strips of the same width and height. This adds a curious temple-like feeling to a very unusual example of Wright's work. Internally, the block piers and walls are repeated and the feeling of the Prairie-Style open space flow is created on the ground floor. The ground floor accommodates a library, billiard room, and the usual living and dining rooms and a kitchen. There are six bedrooms, three on the ground floor and three on the first floor which covers the same area as the dining room, billiard room and kitchen.

The strange character of the house, its massing and extensive floor plan separate it from most of Wright's work around this time and it is possible, as is so often the case with Wright's designs, that it reflects some reservations in his relationship with his cousin.

continued from page 59

recognized to the extent that it deserves when assessing Wright's achievement. One reason for this must be that there are, of course, no photographs of unbuilt works to give a real sense of public identity to the project, only drawings, sketches and plans not often available to the general reader or, if they were, not easily comprehended or fully appreciated. This is singularly unfortunate since some of his more inventive and forward-thinking projects on a larger scale never got past the drawing-board stage. One or two have been completed since his death, however, such as the Marin County Civic Center north of San Francisco and the Guggenheim Museum in New York. As recently as 1995 a design by Wright as interpreted by Taliesin Architects, inheritors of Wright's practice, was commenced at Madison, Wisconsin for a civic complex known as Monona Terrace, on the shore of Lake Monona, carrying echoes of the low arches of Marin County.

The Guggenheim Museum is an example of the development of an idea which originated at the same time as the National Life skyscraper. In an earlier project Wright had conceived the idea of a curved roadway system to follow contours in determining the nature of a large housing scheme and, in 1925, for the entrepreneur Gordon Strong, he adapted this for a double-spiral reinforced concrete motor ramp to a viewing platform on the top of a mountain as an attraction to a holiday resort to be known as the Automobile Objective and Planetarium. This is an early use of the concept of form following motion (an adaptation of Louis Sullivan's more embracing 'Form Follows

Function' adage) which was realized in the descending ramp of the more publicly important Guggenheim design. Despite another serious fire at Taliesin, 1925 was a good year for Wright. More importantly, he had a daughter by Olgivanna and an elegant book devoted to his work was published by the German firm of Wendingen, appraising Wright's influence on European architecture. The author was J. J. P. Oud, an architect member of De Stijl, one of the most important modern art and architectural movements of the early years of the century and both the interest of the author and the book itself indicate the increasing recognition that Wright was beginning to acquire among contemporary European architects, notably in Germany, Holland and Belgium.

Another imaginative project was considered at this time which failed to materialize. A Protestant minister, for whom Wright had already designed a house, which also had not been built, conceived the grandiose notion of an enormous temple of religions, to be the largest religious structure in the world. Although one may be thankful that the money for it was never raised, Wright's sketches for it are interesting and, to some degree, were adapted for a later building, the Beth Sholom Synagogue (1954) in Philadelphia. He envisaged a gigantic pyramid rising 1450ft (442m) over a honeycomb agglomeration of separate chapels or worship centres for different world faiths surrounding a central meeting space. The pyramid was to be covered in double-layered glass over its steel frame and was designed to gleam at night like an immense diamond, producing a feeling of mystical other-worldliness. Imaginative and inventive it may have been, but its principle interest lies, perhaps, in the reminder it gives of another of Wright's early preoccupations deriving from a childhood experience – the Froebel building bricks – which helped foster his continuing interest in basic geometric volumes (in this instance the honeycomb hexagon), an interest which was later to be central to his ideas on design.

The years 1926 and 1927 were dominated by worries for Wright and Olgivanna as a result of the monstrous machinations of Miriam who still pursued him, succeeding in reducing Wright to near despair. He was forced to sell some of his treasured possessions, including Japanese prints, was nearly dispossessed of his home by creditors and was eventually forced to go into hiding with Olgivanna and his illegitimate daughter. He had remained on friendly terms with some of his earlier clients (a tribute both to their satisfaction with his work and a belief in his cause) and they got together to rescue him, forming Frank Lloyd Wright Incorporated, paying off all his debts and giving him a personal stipend. In return, the corporation assumed the ownership of his assets and earnings. It was a traumatic period for the new family and at Olgivanna's urging Wright turned his attention to writing and lecturing. He wrote articles for the architectural press, lectured extensively and began work on his autobiography.

During this time the rebuilding of Taliesin II after the fire of 1925 continued and the virtually new house became Taliesin III. In 1927 Wright received another large commission, San Marcos-in-the-Desert, a complex of a hotel and several houses at Chandler, Arizona for Dr. Alexander Chandler. There was time, before the effects of the Depression of 1929 wiped out the project, for very detailed drawings to be made and for Wright to build the nearby Ocotillo Camp, constructed mainly of wood and canvas, from which to mastermind the ill-fated project and which became the basis for Taliesin West built ten years later on a

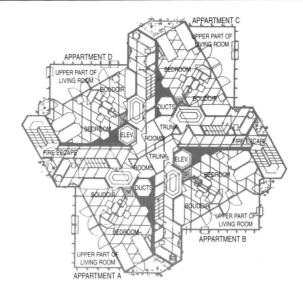

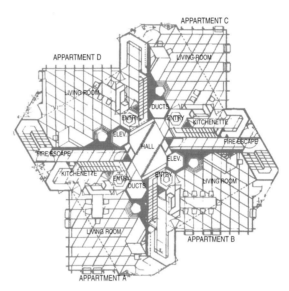

grander scale as a more permanent structure near Phoenix, Arizona. This became the headquarters for Wright's work and private life until he died.

Divorce from Miriam Noel freed Wright to marry Olgivanna and with the baby, Iovanna, and Olgivanna's daughter by her first marriage,

St. Mark's Tower, New York City (1929)
Project.

The fascination of this unexecuted design, intended for the grounds of the old St. Mark's church in the Bowery, is the ingenuity that Wright displays at this early stage in the development of modern architectural structures. Using cantilevers, the tower is constructed of two-floor (duplex) apartments in which the floors are partially skewed to provide a polygonal plan for the 22-floor tower. Wright described his design as a 'taproot' system where the foundations were sunk deeply into the ground and the whole structure cantilevered from the steel and concrete core. Although the tower would have carried some of the particular decorative elements characteristic of Wright, which to some extent would have obscured its very modern conception, the design is a reflection of Wright's dictum that one should build 'in the nature of the materials'. This includes the new as much as the traditional.

House on the Mesa, Denver, Colo. (1931)
Project Model.

The model for the house below was exhibited in the Museum of Modern Art's Exhibition in New York and, as Henry-Russell Hitchcock has pointed out, when shown in conjunction with the modern European architects it reveals 'how much the "old master" was a master'. The design was appropriately modified four years later in Falling Water.

S. C. Johnson and Son Administration Building, Racine, Wis. (1936)

The Johnson Wax Building, as it is more familiarly known, is Wright's second important statement about the nature of office buildings and comes more than 30 years after the first, the Larkin Building (1904). Although a more sophisticated structure – Wright called it 'streamlined' – there are many similarities, not the least being the large open working and clerical area found in each building. In the Johnson Wax Building the space is embellished with what have become one of the most notable and discussed features in the complex – the mushroom columns. These columns, hollow and made of reinforced concrete, narrow at the base and fanning out to surmounting discs, were considered to be of doubtful strength but tests on one proved that their design could support over five times anything they would be asked to carry – over 50 tons.

Like the Larkin Building, Johnson Wax was inward-looking and hermetic, illumination being provided by skylight Pyrex tubing and interior glass walls through which the light gently permeated but with a pleasing efficiency that was much appreciated by the employees – and by the owners who, as a result, had no difficulty in recruiting staff.

Wright also designed the office furniture, much of it in painted metal, and the rounded end shapes of the desks, for instance, provide a link with the open forest of mushroom columns to provide an echo of the streamlined effect of the whole building with its rounded corners and unfenestrated outer brick walls. The complex included a small theatre, recreation terrace, squash court and a basement carport, also with mushroom roofing.

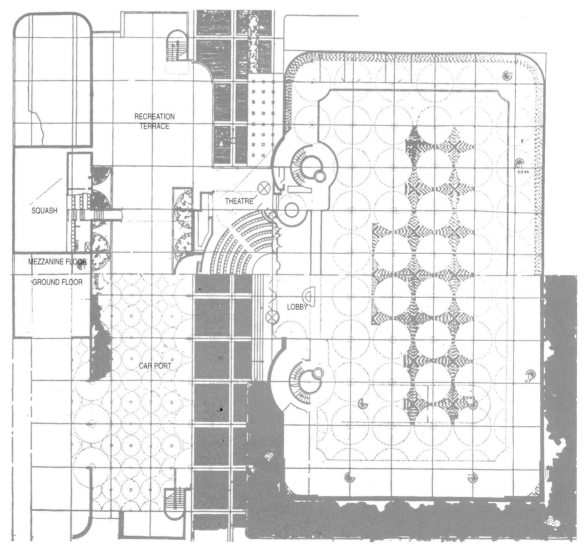

S. C. Johnson and Son Administration Building. Split plan to show ground and mezzanine floor structure.

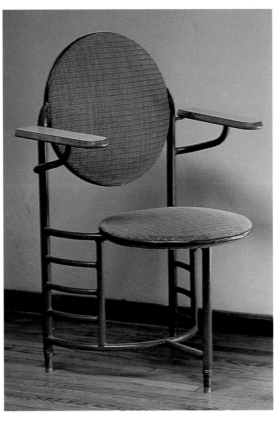

BELOW
Aerial view of the Johnson Building.

Svetlana, they arrived at the desert camp in Arizona where he worked on projects never to be realized because of the Depression. In 1930 he was invited to lecture at Princeton University, the content of which was later published as a book, *Modern Architecture*. He was at the same time working on a model for an exhibition survey with the same title for the Museum of Modern Art (familiarly known as MOMA) in New York. Wright's contribution to the MOMA exhibition was the House on the Mesa project of 1931 (page 67) which featured reinforced concrete cantilevers. In the same year Chicago was planning an exhibition called 'A Century of Progress', which failed to include work by Wright, and by 1934 five years had elapsed since Wright had had a single design erected. He was already 67 years old and it appeared to most observers that his creative career was effectively at an end.

In fact Wright was at the beginning of the most significant period of his long career. Many of his best known buildings were designed, conceived and built in the next decade. In 1932 Wright had organized the Taliesin Fellowship, an architectural workshop later to be located at Taliesin West, for which a modest fee was charged to residential apprentices who followed a varied programme of studio and practical work which included the construction of new buildings for the apprentices

continued on page 76

S. C. Johnson and Son Administration Building, Racine, Wis. (1936)

Two views of the main work space.

Herbert F. Johnson House, 'Wingspread', Wind Point, near Racine, Wis. (1937)

This large mansion, which Wright designed for his Johnson Wax client, is familiarly known as Wingspread and its plan as revealed by the aerial view (opposite below) does indeed suggest a spreadeagled bird although the complex is so extended that this is not immediately obvious as the crossing core of the building rises above the wings and in its form suggests the bridge of a stately ship. However, Wright himself called it a 'wigwam'. The living quarters are arranged arround the massive central chimney structure and consist of a large hall, music room, library and dining area. Each of the wings have separate functions, master bedrooms in one, children's playroom and bedrooms in another, guest rooms and garages in the third, and servants' quarters and services in the fourth.

The suggestion of a ship is emphasized internally by the spiral staircase (opposite top) that rises through the living area to an observatory on the roof. The house is so large, covering in all over 14000sq ft (1300sq m) that when the philanthropic owner founded the Wingspread Foundation it eventually became a conference centre.

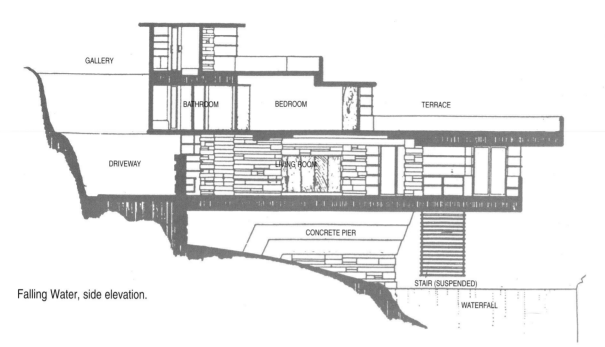

Falling Water, side elevation.

Edgar J. Kaufmann Snr. House, 'Falling Water', Bear Run, Penn. (1936)

Of all Wright's extensive output, two buildings are universally and uniquely linked with his name. People who know little or nothing of his achievements will think immediately of Falling Water and the Guggenheim Museum whenever his name is mentioned. Much controversy has surrounded the museum design but Falling Water was from the beginning recognized as a landmark of modern architecture and a work of genius. It realized, in a very different setting, the ideas implicit in the House on the Mesa in a highly dramatic and original combination of modern technology encompassed within a natural setting. The romantic notion of a house sitting over a waterfall, evoking the poetic imagery of Wordsworth as well as Rousseau and the concept of the natural man, while at the same time being wholly integrated with the scientific technology of a modern age, is a daring and modern concept. Who else but Wright could have cantilevered the house so that it sits right over the waterfall – so far indeed that the waterfall is audible rather than visible. However, it is designed to be seen from the woods and rocks below the house and it is from this viewpoint – and only here – that the audacity of the architecture can be fully appreciated. There is sheer magic, fully appreciated by Wright himself as well as his client, in the relationship of the jutting balcony terrace to its sylvan setting.

It was like a beginning and an end, or rather an end and a beginning because it appeared at a stage in Wright's life when he was regarded as still important but passé, whereas subsequent events proved that he was at the beginning of the most fertile and creative stage in his long career, this building being a token of intent and belief in the future.

The commission to build the house resulted from a trip made by Edgar Kaufmann Jnr. to Taliesin to join the Fellowship, who, on his return home, discussed Wright with his father. Edgar Kaufmann Snr. had been contemplating a weekend retreat to enable him to escape the business world and live a simple rural life in a suitably idyllic setting. He envisaged a 'log cabin in the wilds' solution and the building that Wright proposed came as a considerable shock to him, particularly in its use of concrete rather than local timber and stone. Relations were at times somewhat strained but Wright succeeded in convincing Kaufmann that things should be done his way and the result is one of the best known private houses in the world. So much so that when Kaufmann Jnr. eventually inherited the house it was already a besieged national monument and, resigned to the inevitable, he gave it to a nature conservancy organization. The setting is beautifully preserved but questions regarding the structure of the house are now arising.

The structure itself is a study in balanced oppositions: the horizontal forms of the concrete cantilevered balcony and canopies is in contrast to the vertical masonry pylons of local stone, helping to lock the balcony already linked into the solid rock; the pylons, rectangular, massive and unmoving against the also vertical but delicate motion of the surrounding trees; the flowing water and the static house; all these factors can be discussed *ad infinitum* but the emotions evoked by the place are the most difficult of all to describe.

The house is on three levels and the main floor consists mainly of a single open space flowing from living room to balcony and back towards the kitchen and services. The upper floor consists of bedrooms, bathrooms and two terraces while the smaller top floor has one bedroom, a gallery and a terrace. The side elevation shows the extent to which the main and upper floors are cantilevered.

Internally the exploration of oppositions is continued in, for instance, the combination of a feeling of security with a sense of open freedom against the dense wilderness outside. But even this internal freedom to wander through the large living space is in striking contrast to the narrow, dark and small spaces within the core of the house.

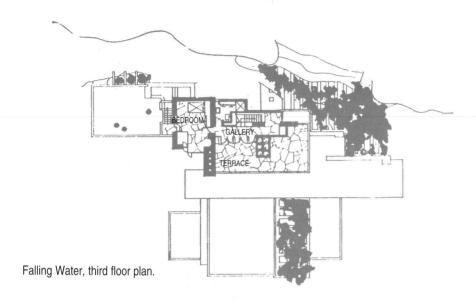

Falling Water, third floor plan.

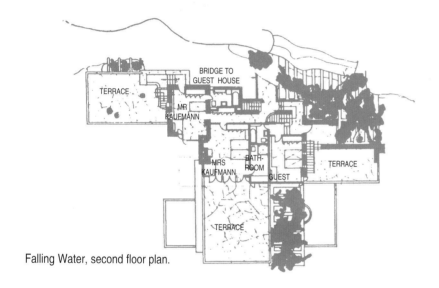

Falling Water, second floor plan.

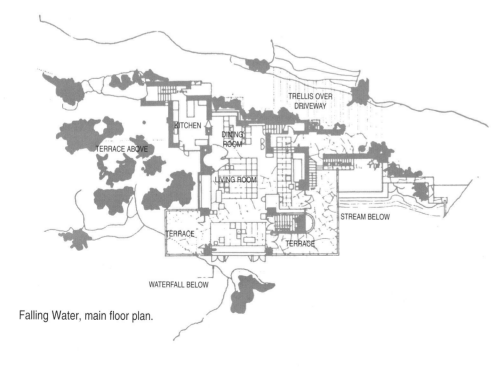

Falling Water, main floor plan.

continued from page 71

themselves. It might be noted that the programme bore similarities to the Gurdjieff Project near Paris in which Olgivanna had earlier participated. Free from the demands of a current and ongoing building programme, Wright devoted time to writing and the first version of his *An Autobiography* appeared in 1932, a much slimmer volume than the later and revised editions but recognized as a more cogent, less wordy exposition of his philosophy and architectural principles and one that was most attractive to young aspirants. It was a source of inspiration for many of his students. He also published *The Disappearing City* which considered the sociological changes that technology had wrought and would be introduced into a changing world. He believed that these changes could not be averted but that with care and planning they could offer an increasingly satisfying *modus vivendi*. It was an optimistic message and he was invited to present his vision of an architectural future at the Rockefeller Center, New York. In preparing his presentation he realized that his ideas might most effectively be expressed visually. He had his students make a model of an urban location four miles square (10sq km) which he called Broadacre City (1934) and which contained a great range of different types of buildings and many of Wright's own building designs were incorporated. When, in the middle of the Depression the model was first exhibited, its vision of a future life inspired hopeful anticipation, stimulating broad-based discussion, not only among the general public but also in the studios at Taliesin where the students were being encouraged to see the role of architecture in a new civilizing and cultural light.

For a few years before the MOMA exhibition of 1932, and its highly significant and influentially distracting offshoot, the Hitchcock/Johnson book *The International Style: Architecture Since 1922,* a forceful debate (not entirely dissimilar to the Battle of the Styles mentioned earlier) began concerning the relationship between architecture and the machine. In *Technics and Civilization* published in 1934, Lewis Mumford, a keenly alert and intelligent architectural and cultural observer, identified the issue. Firstly, he said, it was necessary to assimilate the machine and to accept 'the essence of objectivity, impersonality, neutrality' which it personified after which a 'diminution of the machine' should occur. The International Style, then current, had been a proponent of the machine and according to Wright had resulted in an impoverished and arid architecture, bereft of spirit. In lectures and writings at this time he expressed his concern, if not dismay, at the danger of imagining that only one proper approach to architectural design was correct or acceptable. He called the International Style as seen in the exhibition a 'new eclecticism',

**Herbert Jacobs House,
Westmorland, near Madison, Wis.
(1937)**

One of the first of the so-called
Usonian houses that Wright intended
to be low cost and widely built
throughout local communities. The
Jacobs house carries most of the
Wrightian characteristics of these
houses. It is single storey and stands
on a concrete base with heating ducts
below, familiar from the Prairie Style,
and this continued in the horizontal
boarding, reminiscent of the log cabin.
The boards were used both internally
and externally with a plywood screen
between. The flat roof with extended
eaves incorporates heavy wood
beams. The brick-built kitchen and
bathroom rise above the roof to
provide ventilation.

The plan is L-shaped and living,
dining rooms and bedrooms all face
onto the partially enclosed garden.
There is a car port at one end of the
long arm and a study at the other. The
house is without frills and looks what it
is, a practical utilitarian dwelling.

All Usonian houses were intended
to be low priced and the Jacobs house
was budgeted at $4,500. Much of the
actual building work was undertaken
by the Jacobs family themselves.
Wright himself called the house Usonia
One and it proved to be a prototype for
many more such buildings, only some
of them by Wright.

a commonplace formula that anyone could imitate. What he, with some sympathizers, was calling for was an architecture of spirit, responding without formulism to the individual needs of each commission – in short, an essentially American originality. Although he was nearly 70 years old he seemed inspired by a new enthusiasm.

The Broadacre City model may have had something to do with Wright's new lease of life. Between the years 1934-36 it has often been noted that four very different design programmes, which have since become world-famous, were in preparation, including what is perhaps Wright's best known work, Falling Water, at Bear Run, Pennsylvania. The other three were the Johnson Wax Administration Building, Racine, Wisconsin, the Hanna House and the first Jacobs House, important as the beginning of a sequence of inexpensive DIY houses of ingenious simplicity known as Usonian (United States of North America). They confirmed the return of Wright's vitality and heralded the last great creative stage in his career.

Edgar J. Kaufmann commissioned Wright to build a house in a dramatic wooded setting where the land fell away and a stream called Bear Run ran through the site. Known as Falling Water, for obvious reasons, it was built as a weekend and holiday retreat for city dwellers rather than for permanent occupation and this had some effect on the character of the design. The site provided a sylvan setting for modern technology since Wright employed reinforced concrete, cantilevered (as it had been in the House on the Mesa), but here seemingly more precariously, boldly – even daringly – jutting out over a waterfall. The cantilever was anchored to a rock core on three layers. It was an innovative and brilliant design in a location of outstanding scenic beauty which allowed Wright to achieve a harmonious counterpoint between nature and modern technology.

Following Falling Water, Wright designed Kaufmann Jnr's office in the Kaufmann store in Pittsburgh and this is now on display in the Victoria and Albert Museum in London. For S. C. Johnson and Son he was at the same time working on the much larger project for offices to accommodate executive and clerical staff. The building is low, spread out and without exterior windows, light being introduced through skylights and clerestory strips. The most dramatic element is the interior open plan for the secretarial staff in which a small forest of mushroom-like columns, which have become a famous part of the whole complex, proliferate. Ten years after the first building the dominating research tower was added

Edgar J. Kaufmann Jnr. Office, Kaufmann Department Store, Pittsburgh, Penn. (1937) (Now installed in the Victoria and Albert Museum, London.)

At the same time as Wright was working on Falling Water he designed Kaufmann a new office for his store. This was the year of the first Usonian house and Wright was preoccupied with simple and inexpensive solutions. The result was an office of natural cedar plywood for the walls used for decorative effect to produce a highly unusual and successful interior, also partly inspired by Wright's Japanese experience. The furniture, in character with the room, has some similarity to the designs he made for the Lloyd Lewis House. The textiles were all also designed by Wright, fearful of the use of commercial design, and their production was supervised by Loja Saarinen, wife of the Finnish architect Eliel Saarinen, and someone in whom Wright had great confidence.

Two examples of chairs designed for the Hanna House.

Paul R. Hanna House, 'Honeycomb House', Palo Alto, Calif. (1937)

Paul and Jean Hanna were young academics and when Paul was given a faculty post at Stanford University in 1935 they asked Wright to design a new house for them. They were already familiar with his work and had visited Taliesin so they were able to cooperate with him throughout the design stages. The association appears to have been successful and resulted in a fine and innovative house known as the Honeycomb House, the design being based on a hexagon. This caused the builders considerable problems since they had to use 120- rather than the usual 90-degree angles. Wright also designed special furniture and fittings in keeping with the hexagonal module.

The house was extensively remodelled in the 1950s as the needs of the family changed. The grown-up children left and a guesthouse and workshop were added. The interior was altered to reduce the number of rooms and increase the size of some. The garden had matured over the years to become one of the finest parts of the complex which included a large lava stone garden urn which the Hannas had brought from the Imperial Hotel, Tokyo, before its demolition. The house is now owned and maintained by the University.

Taliesin West, Scottsdale, near Phoenix, Ariz. (1937-59)

Wright's passion for the desert spaces of the south-west of the United States developed from his encounter with Dr. Alexander Chandler and the designs for the intended complex at San Marcos-in-the-Desert (page 47) with the nearby Ocotillo Camp constructed to prepare the plans for it. From this came the new Taliesin, a more permanent and substantial structure than Ocotillo and including Wright's increasing interest in new forms derived from simple or complicated geometrical shapes. The use of hexagonal blocks has been noted in the Hanna house and at Taliesin the right angle was allied to the 60/30-degree division. The use of battered (angled) walls rather than vertical, together with single-angled roofs carry this variation from the normal which is more readily apparent on the plan.

The complex sits tight and low in the flat desert and echoes the low rise of the background hills. The heavy desert stone walls and the redwood beam frames reflect the strong continuing interest Wright had in the materials he used. The white canvas covering repeats the tent-like effect that characterized Ocotillo.

The plan reveals the strong single directional nature of the complex at the core of which was the great workroom over which Wright presided. Integrated with the linear thrust was a crossover 60/30-degree angling, adding a dynamic sense of movement to the apprentices' court and dormitories. The angled entrance lane is dominated by a pylon and fountain designed by Wright.

The buildings were subject to extensive alteration while Wright lived and were the centre of the Taliesin Fellowship which became, as the apprentices were dispersed throughout the United States and Europe, even more famous than the original first Taliesin at Spring Green. It remains a potent image of Wright's ability to create a modern architecture which is outside the familiar aesthetic although parallel to it.

and its rounded corners suggested to some observers an echo of the Johnson Wax products themselves. Whether or not this was a conscious intention on Wright's part, it does seem to reflect, as indeed does the whole complex, something of the character of the company's merchandise. This subliminal identification is frequently encountered in Wright's work, for example the Larkin Building, and reflects the subjective, artistic core of his designs.

The strong resurgence of Wright's career continued and in 1937 a further commission for a house for Herbert F. Johnson, which Wright claimed was his last Prairie house, was built at Wind Point north of Racine. It was known as 'Wingspread' and the name reflects its large scale design over a spreading cruciform plan. Although a lavish and elegant concept, it is considered by most commentators as less important in Wright's creative *oeuvre* than the two smaller houses mentioned above, the Paul R. Hanna House, Palo Alto, California and the first Herbert Jacobs House at Madison, Wisconsin.

The development of an inexpensive building programme had always interested Wright, as the Usonian designs indicate, and the first Jacobs house is a single-commission example of what he had hoped would be adopted widely for large scale housing schemes. Designed on an L-shaped plan, rather than the cruciform he usually employed, it provides immediate access to the garden from living room and bedrooms, as well as other original features discussed elsewhere. Other individual examples of Usonian-type houses were built (in his autobiography he claims 27 in '17 Usonian States'). In 1939, two further important manifestations of his commitment to the idea of producing simple inexpensive, small and convenient houses, were the Rosenbaum House in Florence, Alabama, which Hitchcock describes as a larger and more perfect version of the first Jacobs House, and the compact masterpiece for two art teachers, Katherine Winkler and Alma Goetsch, who were faculty members of Michigan State University, Lansing. A group of professors had commissioned Wright to design seven houses for a site that they had purchased but, in the event, only this one was built, although the model for the whole scheme was exhibited in the Museum of Modern Art, New York in 1940.

The Paul Hanna House was built in the grounds of Stanford University, California and was of a very different design, being constructed on a grid of hexagons which introduced the 60/30-degree ratio found in some of Wright's earlier projects of the 1920s and which evolved out of his fascination with geometric forms. He believed that this hexagonal module offered the opportunity for a more flexible internal relationship than the more familiar rectangular module. He used the triangular

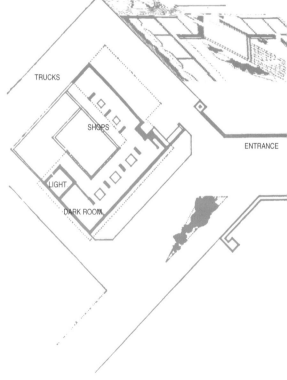

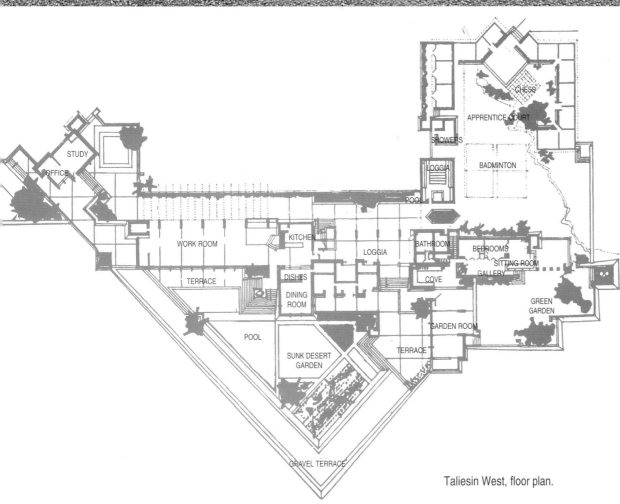

Taliesin West, floor plan.

Project design for a 'House for a Family of $5,000-$6,000 Income' for *Life* **Magazine (1938)**

The *Life* design carries some Prairie characteristics but is essentially an enlarged version of the Usonian type. Notably, there is considerable emphasis on the flat slab roof and cantilevered overhanging concrete eaves. The published designs were almost precisely used for the Bernard Schwartz House, Two Rivers, Wisconsin, in the following year. The ground floor provides a large open-plan recreation and sitting room with a dining area, office and workspace as a small complex off the recreation area. The upper semi-mezzanine floor has two bedrooms and servant quarters and a master bedroom suite on the lower floor. The house is of brick and concrete.

formula for the plan of Taliesin and later for the
Unitarian Church (1947) at Shorewood Hills,
Wisconsin. The Hanna house, on an elevated site,
operated efficiently for the professional academic
parents, their three children, and the many students
from Stanford who were constant visitors. It could
be said that it presented something of a problem
for the builders when they came to connect the
unusual elements and angles together structurally
and the help of the Hannas was called in to resolve
difficulties as they arose.

Most importantly for Wright himself, the
building of the new headquarters for the
Fellowship was progressing and Taliesin West,
which was subsequently to become the centre and
core of his later life, came into being at Scottsdale,
Arizona, becoming even more famous than its
earlier namesakes as it was added to and the
original temporary materials were replaced by
wood, stone and concrete. Although many
masterpieces were produced during the course of
his long career, the name Taliesin recurs
throughout and is, of course, a reminder of
Wright's maternal Welsh ancestry.

Wright had also started another large project at
this time, a campus for Florida Southern College at
Lakeland. He considered the usual pattern of
academic building inherited from the widespread
increase in new state-funded European universities
and seemingly representative of academic
excellence in visible form, to be inappropriate for
the youth of America (an incidental reminder of
his concern to express essentially American
qualities and characteristics in his work). Even as
an engineering student he had expressed his

continued on page 92

Katherine Winkler and Alma Goetsch House, Okemos, Mich. (1939)

Widely recognized as the most
successful of the Usonian houses, the
simple sophistication and clarity of the
design for the Winkler/Goetsch house,
together with the refined use of
materials, internally and externally,
singles it out for this assessment. The
house was the only one executed out
of the seven planned by a group of
professors at the University of
Michigan. The single-storey, strongly
directional design is built on a level-
ground site and with the usual
concrete base. Although not as
evident here, the house in brick and
concrete rises in linked blocks
externally which lends it a singularly
modern 1930s European box
appearance contradicted internally by
a free-flowing space with no sense of
constriction in what is after all a small,
two-bedroom house. In a wooded
location the ground dips away from
the studio/living area revealing a
pleasant prospect of trees.

George D. Sturges House, Brentwood Heights, Calif. (1939)

The small Sturges house looks surprisingly sturdy and solid on its steep site. The extended cedarwood-covered concrete cantilever recalls Falling Water in its boldness. Essentially a single-storey structure, it nevertheless appears to rise through several levels from a solid brick base which contains a workshop, through the main floor with its jutting cantilevered terrace and open canopy of redwood to an upper smaller terrace. The sharpness of the main floor cantilever is softened by the inverted wooden bracket. The living space consists of a living room with a dining area, two bedrooms and a workspace.

The small scale but bold treatment shows the amount of variety that Wright was able to introduce in a house that is in fact Usonian.

Lloyd Lewis House, Libertyville, Ill. (1940)

Apart from the Usonian designs which maintained a family similarity and were small in scale and relatively inexpensive, the variety of the houses Wright built makes him one of the most inventive of all domestic architects. His houses range in scale from the large mansions, elaborately detailed, such as Wingspread for Herbert Johnson to the compact Edwin Cheney house.

In Wright's *An Autobiography* there is an amusing and illuminating account of his friendship with Lloyd Lewis and his wife Kathryn. He describes Lewis as his 'own dear friend' and outlines the discussions and difficulties that accompanied the building of this larger than usual Usonian house, notably of the fireplace that refused to draw – 'one out of three thousand, to tell truth, that did not draw'. Lewis was a journalist, writer and, by the time the house was built, the editor of a local paper, and enjoyed the house as did most of their visitors. One, Alexander Woollcott, said that the house 'uplifts the heart and refreshes the spirit'.

The Lloyd Lewis house, built on a bank of the Des Plaines River, has both its base and core of brick and although essentially a one-storey house, the main floor is raised above the damp riverside on brick piers with a cantilevered concrete terrace surmounted with a glass screen to protect against encroaching trees and river mists. The design is strongly linear and Hitchcock describes it as having 'the handsomest and most harmonious furnishing of any of Wright's later houses'.

**Ann Pfeiffer Chapel, Florida
Southern College, Lakeland, Fla.
(1940). Plan and elevation.**

When Wright was given the
opportunity to plan the entire college
campus for a then small and
unremarkable coeducational
Methodist college dating from 1885,
he obtained what proved to be his
most extensive executed commission
since the Imperial Hotel of over 20
years earlier. The college's own
official leaflet, with generous
enthusiasm, claims that the result is
'the world's most beautiful campus,
designed by the greatest architect of
all time'.

Wright found the project
particularly attractive since it gave him
an opportunity to realize his theories
as to what constituted the perfect
environment for effective education –
that it should not be psychologically
historicist, dominated by the European
classical or medievalist architectural

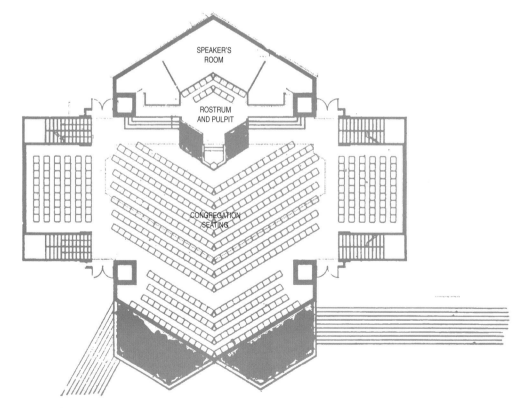

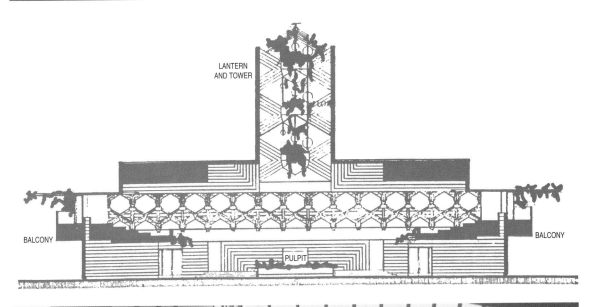

LANTERN AND TOWER

BALCONY

BALCONY

PULPIT

patterns. Sixteen buildings were planned for the site – an extensive orange grove on flat lakeside land with no helpful natural feature to which the architect could relate and, remembering Falling Water, inimical to Wright's intentions. His design had to occupy and determine the whole area. He planned covered walkways to provide protection from the summer tropical heat and heavy rains in winter and to link the activity areas which would nestle among the citrus trees with low white buildings surrounded by terraces. One of the more dramatic and theatrical features was a water dome fountain which never in the event worked and was later demolished. Not all the other structures were completed but those that were included the circular library, an industrial arts centre and the Pfeiffer Chapel which, among the orange trees and the low buildings, dominated the complex on its central site with its high steel tower intended to provide a source of filtered light for the interior.

The plan of the chapel is almost hexagonal but two rectangular side ears offer extra seating while the rostrum is hexagonal. There is no natural rock on the site and the buildings are mainly of concrete, including the chapel. Money was short and much of the construction work was undertaken by the students who obtained a partial reduction of their tuition fees in return for mixing concrete and laying blocks and slabs for the connecting paths.

Herbert Jacobs House II, Middleton, Wis. (1946).

By the time the Jacobs family was ready to commission a second house from Wright, he had developed a fascination for geometric basic forms, for example the hexagon for the Hanna House. The first Jacobs Usonian house was an L-shaped single-storey inexpensive structure and the new house was also intended to be inexpensive so that, again, the family could undertake much of the building work themselves. The circle was the basic form for the new house which Wright called a 'solar hemicyclo' and which was placed on a small hilltop site into which the house was set. It was larger than the first house designed to accommodate Herbert and Katherine Jacobs and their three young children.

continued from page 85

detestation of the visible trappings of academic classicism in architectural forms, the column, pilaster, cornice and 'all the architectural paraphernalia of the defunct Renaissance' and his designs were both elegant and refreshingly uncluttered with historicism. Wright was always seeking new creative solutions and the peculiar circumstances of this commission, where a shortage of cash enabled the students to defray part of their tuition fees by undertaking building work themselves, resulted in a design composed of cast concrete building blocks, echoing the earlier textile blocks but providing larger-scale decorative forms. This was planning on a scale unusual in American universities which, unplanned and with private funding for individual buildings, like Topsy, just growed. Wright planned a campus which was intended to be so complete as to be virtually unchangeable. Not all the planned buildings were erected so that the overall intention of providing a number of units connected by a covered esplanade did not materialize. Of the individual buildings, the Ann Pfeiffer Chapel is the most visible landmark.

In January 1938 the important magazine *Architectural Forum* was entirely devoted to a survey of Wright's work and in the same year *Life* magazine commissioned a design for a 'House for a Family of 5,000-6,000 Dollars Income' which, not surprisingly, achieved wide attention and helped to make Wright a household name. Amid widespread publicity, Wright came to London in the following year to give four lectures to specialist audiences. Wright had carefully considered what he would say and the lectures when published later in the same year as *An Organic Architecture* are generally thought to be a most effective statement of his own philosophy.

It is hardly surprising that at this period in his life Wright should have presented a considerable problem to his contemporaries. On the one hand he was world-famous and much revered; his architecture was original and personal but not modern in the then *avant garde* White Box ethos. On the other hand, if he could not be accommodated into the current aesthetic neither could he be marginalized. Following his outburst against the International Style exhibition in 1932, he was accused of a U-turn in that, having led architecture to a new freedom, he now wished to return it to the shackles of tradition. In a lecture delivered later in 1955 Philip Johnson, one of the joint authors of *The International Style*, expressed the position thus: 'Frank Lloyd Wright is our Michelangelo. One day, more than fifty years ago, he founded modern architecture, and he has been founding styles ever since, but with ever decreasing relevance.' '... architecture today is a style, and Frank Lloyd Wright, though he has been much influenced by it, is not part of it.' Johnson, speaking in 1955, was of course still equating

modern architecture with the International Style – to that extent he was undoubtedly correct.

Although the Second World War began in 1939, it was not until the end of 1941 that America entered. Wright was not prepared to participate and, since most of his apprentices were away, the war years at Taliesin were not very productive. In projects started in 1940 Wright opened a new and controversial direction which has seemed to contradict the whole organic aesthetic that he had positively declared in *An Organic Architecture*. He introduced a single geometric form to provide the basic dominant mass of a building. Instead of the flowing space, covered but not confined by the roof and limited but not defined by walls, he now began to choose geometric forms such as circles, triangles or rectangles to identify and control the whole image of the building: he also used complementary parts of geometric elements, such as an arc in a circular structure. In one design, for instance, the Roy Petersen Project of 1941, a large equilateral triangle was introduced. The house was not built but the adapted design was used effectively in the Palmer House (1950) at Ann Arbor, Michigan. In another example he proposed a double arc which was used in a number of houses such as the Andrew B. Cooke House, Virginia Beach (1953). His intention, it appears, was to express the dominance of the vitality which he discerned in the purity of geometric forms over intellectually constructed abstraction; of personality over theory. Although this may seem to be a somewhat obscure and abstruse intention, much at variance with his previous 'organic' philosophy and architectural achievements, he still succeeded in finding a number of clients who seemed satisfied with his designs. Nevertheless, the significant change in direction that this represents, in a man who was already in his mid-70s has always been widely debated, often being seen as a diminution of his faculties. His later achievements belie this assessment but it has to be acknowledged that the change has given some credence to claims that he jettisoned his humanism for form's sake.

During the war years, discussions took place and designs were produced for a second house for Herbert Jacobs and his increasing family, the small earlier house having become inadequate. Agreed in 1945, the house was finished two years later. Following his new direction it was in the form of what Wright called a solar hemicyclo set into the hillside facing south and constructed as a single storey. Not one of his magnificent houses, and of inexpensive construction, it nevertheless provided a satisfying sense of womblike privacy and enveloping homeliness for the Jacobs family. If it proves anything it is that Wright's use of geometric basic forms, in this case the circle, did not inhibit his creative use of them.

The Jacobs had undertaken much of the

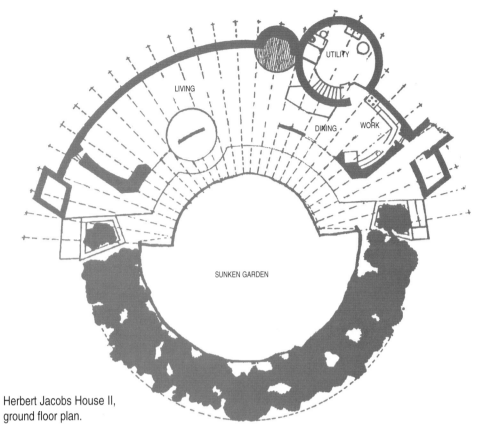

Herbert Jacobs House II,
ground floor plan.

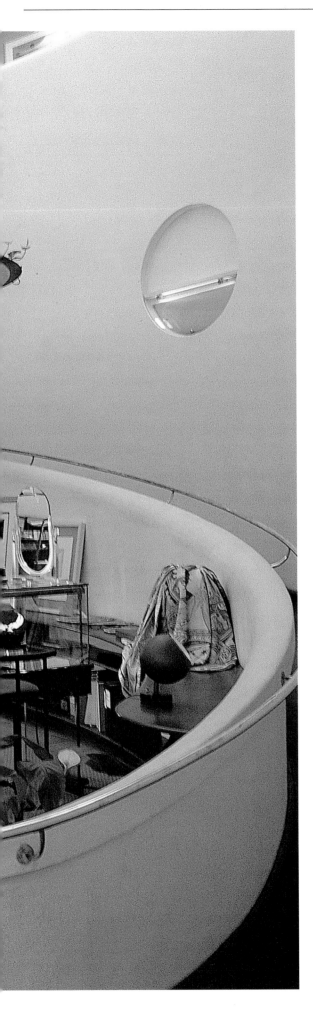

building work themselves in order to reduce costs and the Douglas Grants, for their house at Cedar Rapids, Iowa (1947) also did much of the interior work themselves. The design took the form of a long rectangle leading to a two-storey living room. The result was a simple and satisfying home for the Grant family.

Solomon Guggenheim first contacted Wright early in the 1940s through the insistence of an extraordinary lady with whom he was much infatuated, the baroness Hilla Rebay von Ehrenwiesen, a painter and art fanatic with a passion for abstract painting. The story of his conversion from being a collector of old masters to a devotee of modern art is a well known and fascinating one. The result was one of Wright's most controversial works, the Guggenheim Museum, New York.

By the time of Wright's involvement with him, Solomon R. Guggenheim had amassed an extensive collection of modern art works, through Hilla Rebay's influence particularly abstract and abstractionist examples, and Wright – Solomon's contemporary, only six years his junior – was brought in to design an appropriate museum to house them. The eventual result is one of the most debated and significant buildings of the century. It sits like a small snail in the vertical Manhattan forest of what Wright called 'abortive boxes endeavouring to look tall'. The museum was incongruous and forceful, impossible to ignore. Guggenheim died before building started but funds had been secured and the museum was erected; however, because changes of policy were made by Guggenheim's executors, the building was skimped and eventually used contrary to the terms of the commission fulfilled by Wright who himself died five months before the museum was opened in October 1959.

The building took the form of an expanded

V. C. Morris Gift Shop, San Francisco, Calif. (1948)

One of the main internal features of this famous shop in San Francisco, Wright's only design in that city, is that it is a prototype for the Guggenheim Museum, which though not yet built had been designed by the time the Morris store was completed. Wright's fascination with the descending circular or curving ramp has already been noted. It predates, in the Gordon Strong design of 1925, for instance, the later interest in geometrical forms seen in the second Herbert Jacobs house. In the Morris shop the two interests are combined in the gently curving ramp in which the store's merchandise is displayed. Other interior features, from the ceiling with its Plexiglas discs which gently filters the light so that no damage is caused to the coloured fabrics displayed within, to the inserted fittings, make the whole interior a memorable aesthetic experience.

Perhaps even more interesting, however, is the exterior flat unfenestrated brick façade broken only by the Richardsonian Romanesque semi-circular arch constructed of four receding bands of brick. The entrance through the arch is divided by a low brick wall with a light banded stone finish and a glass panel on one half while the other half is in the metal gate entrance. It is a startling and impressive solution to the problem of small shop design where the small protected entrance suggests both exclusivity and high value.

Unitarian Church, Shorewood Hills, Wis. (1947)

During his long life Wright designed a number of churches, including the first Unity Temple in Oak Park and, since Wright himself was a Unitarian, it is not surprising that when the Shorewood Hills congregation was determined to have him design its planned new church he acceded, although he was over 70 years old. He took great pains with the design and spent much time on site. The result, it is claimed, possessed an atmosphere of great calm and reverence, a place conducive to quiet worship.

The plan conjoined two triangles of different sizes and the whole structure was covered with a copper roof. Two side wings to the rear house the Sunday School and the service facilities. The great swooping roof rising to a high point invites a comparison, as do others of Wright's houses, to a ship's prow and there is undoubtedly a strong sense of the main front appearing to be urgently surging forward.

spiral ramp narrowing towards the base, or what might be described as an inverted and truncated spiral cone. It should be noted that in his earlier Strong project for a restaurant on a mountain top, he revealed an interest in the spiral form and in the later V. C. Morris Gift Shop in San Francisco (1948) he had used a descending spiral ramp. The four tiers of the Guggenheim were intended to provide a continuous viewing area within a confined volume. The success of the design has been strenuously debated and the building will continue to be considered and evaluated elsewhere: nevertheless, it is interesting to note that the Guggenheim is a design dominated by Wright's own personality, which, when one thinks of his late attachment to the idea of geometric definition, is an interesting, even inspiring example of the imaginative use of a formula by the most unconfinable creative spirit of 20th-century architecture. Only his contemporary, Le Corbusier, approaches him in this respect and Corbusier was too much driven by a desire for consistent rationality, even in such buildings as the Pilgrimage Chapel at Ronchamp, to display the arrogant quirkiness that was Wright's handprint. Perhaps their differences might be expressed as similar temperaments divided by national characteristics.

The achievement of his final years suggests Wright's continuing power to provide unexpected solutions. Two of his later buildings provoke interesting speculation on the extent to which the architect's personal beliefs may inform his designs. Wright's Unitarian background may have made him sympathetic to Unitarianism when he designed the Unity Temple for Oak Park in 1906, but could this also extend to two designs of the mid-1950s, the Beth Sholom Synagogue at Elkins Park, Pennsylvania (1957) and the Annunciation Greek Orthodox Church at Wauwatosa, Wisconsin (1954)? Wright clearly felt equal to the task of creating a satisfying ambience for a faith that was not his own. While both the buildings have dramatic and different outward forms, the internal spaces are physically and emotionally similar. Whether or not the very different structures are appropriate to their individual religious use may be difficult to establish although the decorative elements in the synagogue are said to conform to Jewish symbolism and ritual. Wright no doubt had confidence himself that they would. However, even more effective in use, and perhaps not surprisingly, appears to be the Unitarian Church at Shorewood Hills, Wisconsin (1947), which included an angled shed roof and a great glass window looking out on the greenery beyond. In the event, this building became famous as an unostentatious setting for quiet worship.

In these same years Wright also completed a number of houses among which was the interesting Gillin House at Dallas, Texas (1950) which used

inverted dish forms in a cellular irregular pattern to produce one of his most elaborate mansion houses on the late geometric principle, again confirming that his mind was creatively active and could arrive at design solutions of originality and flexibility within the constraints he had set himself.

In 1951 the American Institute of Architects awarded Wright its Gold Medal, ten years after he had been awarded the Gold Medal of the Royal Institute of British Architects. He was also again accorded an entire issue of *Architectural Forum*. He had triumphantly succeeded in avoiding incorporation within the establishment while at the same time establishing an unassailable position as the greatest native-born American architect of the century. As well as being clearly one of the

greatest creative figures of this century, Wright himself, characteristically, and on several occasions opined that he was the greatest architect that had ever lived. Well, if you don't say it no one can question it, and it certainly puts a thought in the mind. Even after his death, his ability to provide a creative shock continued. His plans for the Marin County Civic Center, designed by 1957 but not completed until 1966, resulted in a commanding multi-arched structure bridging the foothills at San Raphael outside San Francisco which has provoked as much debate as the Guggenheim, seen by some as a grotesquely inflated structure which offends the landscape, but viewed by others as his last great monument, built to his original design and spanning the valley like a magnificent echo of a Roman viaduct.

continued on page 108

Harold C. Price Company Tower, Bartlesville, Okla. (1952)

Wright was approached by Harold Price to design an office building for his oil company and was startled to find a high-rise tower envisaged when he was expecting a low spreading design. Wright's proposal arose from the unexecuted St. Mark's Tower of 1929 with its taproot construction and the Price Tower was a mixed-use office and apartment solution. Price was, however, so attracted by its originality and elegance that not only did he allow Wright to proceed (only reducing the proposed height from 22 to 19 floors) but himself acted as realtor as well as oilman. Wright described the structure as a composite shaft of concrete rising through the floors which were each cantilevered 'similar to the branch of a tree'. The reinforced concrete floors are balanced by the extensive use of copper with its characteristic green colour appearing on canopies, balconies and louvres and the lobby with enamelled metal abstract decoration echoes its effect.

Price was delighted with the tower and he and Wright became close friends, resulting in two houses for the Price family.

Beth Sholom Synagogue, Elkins Park, Penn. (1954)

One of the more interesting aspects of the later designs for public buildings is the variety of form and aesthetic character that Wright produced. Two examples of religious structures executed in the 1950s graphically illustrate the point. The synagogue in Elkins Park was constructed with the full cooperation of the Rabbi; it resulted in a pyramidal building mainly of steel, glass and aluminium supported by a concrete frame, an adaptation from the earlier church for all religions he had designed in which a wigwam-like shape of steel and glass would have sheltered a number of different chapels and temples.

The interior has a tent-like quality with decorative and symbolic elements designed by Wright under the instruction of the Rabbi and other advisers. An entrance vestibule leads to a chapel and two rest rooms while the main auditorium and centre of worship is approached by a flight of stairs directed towards the Ark, which itself is fronted by blocks of seats at different angles determined by the soaring roof and varying floor levels. It seats over 1,000 worshippers.

The translucent roof delivers a soft, variable light during the passage of the day while at night the whole building externally glows with light.

**Annunciation Greek Orthodox
Church, Wauwatosa, Wis. (1956)**

The second religious building, designed at about the same time as the Beth Sholom synagogue, is the Greek Orthodox church which Wright based upon the early forms of the Greek church, the domed central structures and the Greek cross, which provided the ground plan. The dome, although inspired by Byzantine models such as Santa Sophia in Istanbul, is shallower, however, and bears down on the interior rather than receding upwards.

The building is essentially circular and internally a dished bowl-shaped balcony, supported on piers and surrounded by low arches which, in turn, carry the domed roof. As distinct from the triangular basic form of the synagogue, the Greek church is, as already noted, basically circular and the different inspirations for each reflects Wright's conversion to geometric forms. Much discussion has centred on whether Wright discerned his much loved and publicized enthusiasm and devotion to what he called 'organic' architecture in the geometry or whether he had transferred his loyalties. However, these two religious buildings, together with other late work, seem to present a different philosophy from that seen in his early work.

FROM TALIESIN WEST TO THE GUGGENHEIM MUSEUM 1937-1959

Solomon R. Guggenheim Museum, New York City (1946-59)

Something has already been said in the Introduction about the origins and history of the museum; but it should also be noted here that the later stages of the building became a trial and tribulation to Wright in the last years of his life. Eventually, the constant necessity for him to be present on site caused him to take an apartment in the Plaza Hotel, lower down 5th Avenue, cynically dubbed Taliesin East.

The main construction material was concrete in a variety of forms, such as reinforced and sprayed, and it has to be said that the spiral ramp design demanded the manipulatory character of the material. The circular inverted and truncated conical main space was lit by a surmounting dome and the ground floor was left an open circular court. Thus the central volume was an empty drum with artificial light for the descending ramp. The controversial design centred much attendant criticism on the suitability of the ramps as exhibition spaces for paintings. It was also felt that the building would prove too powerful a backdrop for the display of works of art. It is, however, a building that inevitably does evoke strong responses which can only effectively be resolved by a visit. The author confesses to experiencing a certain ambivalence on visiting the museum, his attention divided between the magnificence of what is on display and the individualist power of the structure itself.

THE SOLOMON R GUGGE

Guggenheim Museum: view on ramp.

ABOVE Glass cupola.

Guggenheim Museum,
ground floor plan.

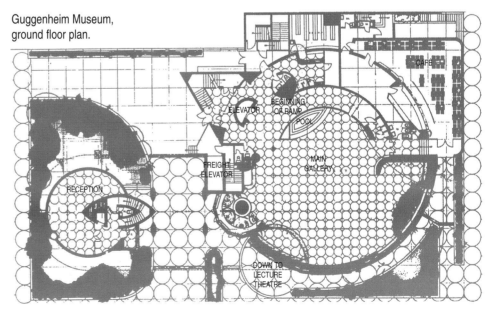

Le Corbusier (Charles-Édouard Jeanneret-Gris) (1887-1965). Chapel of Nôtre-Dame-du-Haut, Ronchamp, France (1951-55)

This chapel which Le Corbusier regarded as his masterwork, carrying his deepest spiritual message, caused incomprehension and dismay among his admirers. It represented a radical departure from what the *British Architect* described as 'the rational principles which are the basis of the modern movement' in that the forms were strongly modelled, the surface textures roughly aggressive and the interior spaces intricately coloured. The whole effect of the building is closer to the Wrightian view than any of the works of his contemporaries and offers a curious sympathy with the Guggenheim Museum which was under construction at the same time.

continued from page 99

Another example of his continuing creative output in the 1950s is the Price Tower, Bartlesville, Oklahoma, erected in 1952. In the event, it turned out to be the only near skyscraper he designed that was actually built. As might be expected, it was of an unusual design, perhaps best seen in the typical floor plan which is a variant of the New York skyscraper project design of 1929 with its ingenious interlocking of duplex apartments on each floor. The tower itself originated from designs for the much earlier 1896 watertower/windmill at Spring Green, Wisconsin, for the Misses Lloyd Jones, an early witness to his independence and originality.

The originality of the design of the Guggenheim Museum reflects many aspects of Wright's character; determined, positive, inflexible when he had made up his mind. Once he had conceived the idea of a continuous spiral ramp discussion had little effect unless it was in support of his own opinion. The particular structural difficulties posed by the use of a conical inverted spiral were determinedly overcome although the question of its appropriateness, crystal clear to Wright, has remained a subject of debate.

It is coincidental and instructive to look at two buildings of other recognized masters of modern architecture completed at around the same time as the Guggenheim Museum. In 1955 Le Corbusier's Pilgrimage Chapel, Nôtre-Dame-du-Haut at Ronchamp in the Vosges region of France was completed. It, too, had an unusual form with a large dark concrete roof overhanging the slanted walls, a formidable entrance with attendant pylons, an apparently random pattern of small fenestration areas filled with coloured glass. In much the same way that the Guggenheim disturbed Wright's adherents, Le Corbusier's friends, supporters of the White Box, found Ronchamp almost incomprehensible while others doubted its appropriateness to its use. If Le Corbusier himself is to be believed, it was a 'sacred task' and he brought something of the zeal of a medieval master mason to its creation. Nevertheless, both buildings have an independent spirit of creativity in common and express a nascent dissatisfaction with the concept of the White Box.

In 1958 Mies van der Rohe completed the elegant and much-admired Seagram Building on Park Avenue, New York which became a paradigm for the great glass-clad steel frame towers that soon spread across America and quickly became a partial alternative to the White Box and an extension of the International Style. The difference between the aesthetic offered by these buildings and the Guggenheim and Ronchamp structures is

obvious. Wright regarded such towers as boring and inartistic. It is just this factor that distinguishes the architecture of Wright, and, incidentally Le Corbusier as well, from the unembellished rectangular form. It is the belief, perhaps inspired by reading Ruskin, that decoration, an art element, is a necessary and appropriate part of the practice of architecture. It is self-evidently not an easy matter to examine without emotional or intellectual involvement but it was so significant to Wright that it must be considered, if only briefly.

It is a common preoccupation of individuals concerned with the nature of architecture to speculate on the degree to which art is necessarily part of architecture. Nikolaus Pevsner, in his *Outline of European Architecture*, distinguishes between building and architecture by asserting that architecture has an additional 'aesthetic' dimension. Explicitly, therefore, he claims that achitecture, always, by its distinction from mere structure must have an art component. The difference between Wright and Mies is the former's belief that art will be a visually evident concommitant of architectural form while Mies believed art to be immanent in structure, proportion and scale which would provide all the aesthetic values it needed. Until the 1960s, most professionals who were part of the modern movement followed Mies. As early as 1928, Lewis Mumford had linked Wright with Le Corbusier, suggesting, surprisingly, that Wright was the successor to Le Corbusier rather than the other way round.

A dictum of Mies's 'Less is More' was translated by Robert Venturi into 'Less is a Bore'. With the emphasis on the latter, he published *Complexity and Contradiction in Architecture* in 1966 and since then there has been an increasing emphasis on what may be called the overt art element. Post-Modernism, as its name implies, is one such development. Seen in the light of this development, the role that Wright ultimately played was central not only to post-1960s modern architecture but also to the later developments of High Tech and Deconstructionist philosophy.

The most superficial reflection on Wright's career, when one remembers that when he was born Richardsonian architecture was the latest thing and by the time he died the most revolutionary modern movement in architectural design had failed to achieve the universal acceptance that its supporters had believed to be inevitable, will establish the relevance of the central core of his faith in the supremacy of artistic creativity. As time passes his own arrogant, aggressive and confident assumption of his own genius can increasingly be seen to be justified. Would that it could happen to us all.

Ludwig Mies van der Rohe (1886-1969) and Philip Johnson 1906- Seagram Building, New York City (1954-58)

An elegant, dignified example of the style that Wright found unacceptable as the only permitted style for a modern architectural solution. Although an obviously carefully considered and highly practical building on a very restricted but commercially desirable site, it appeared to followers of Wright not to express the essential but subjective element of individual personality which Wright and his followers believed to be an important feature of all great architecture. The classical simplicity of the Seagram tower was nevertheless such an inspiration to architects, already somewhat disenchanted with the white concrete box, that it became the model for many 1960s skyscrapers both inside and outside the United States.

CODA

Marin County Civic Center, San Raphael, Calif. (1957-66)

The Civic Center was until recently Wright's last executed design and is also one of his more expansive conceptions, provoking as much comment as any of his works. It looks somewhat like a part design for a city of the future as it spreads across valley and hill as if providing a link to some great underground metropolis. A slender radio pylon soars centrally above what is actually a library centre but looks like a communications futures system under its dome and arches, similar to the Greek church designed at the same time. The low repeating arches, which had become a feature of some of his later work, follow the wings across the valley floor, at the same time evoking an ancient Roman aqueduct. The whole design is clearly dominated by the circular form and reflects Wright's concentration in his later work on the basic geometrical elements which have seemed to many a withdrawal from the mainspring inspiration of most of his work – organic form. Nevertheless, it is too soon to be sure that this work will not serve as inspiration to future designers.

Throughout this book there has been an attempt to present Wright in all the extraordinary variety that his long life and uniquely varied career provided. Much of what he designed was not actually built though even more was. In the study of all the designs, built or not built, the architect that emerges is substantially different from the popular perception both of architects in general and, most importantly, of Wright himself.

He was not merely a professional architect devoted to slavishly carrying out his clients' wishes for commercial reward. That, of course, is not to say that he did not expect to be paid adequately or even generously for his services; but it does suggest that his agenda was more akin to the true creative artist, pursuing his own personal goals in the same way that a painter or composer does, with scant attention to the desires or even the comprehension of his patrons. When Wright felt the need to change direction, he did. Such single-mindedness rarely leads to a quiet life and does not necessarily make for a popular artist. But it does mean that surprise, excitement, revelation and enhancement – what could be called a work of art – may be generated.

Of all the architects of his time, none pursued his Muse more tenaciously or ruthlessly and none achieved a wider remit from her in return. It is difficult to think of any architect who personally added more depth and variety to the architecture of his day and it is well known that he was often

heard to claim that he was the greatest living architect and, perhaps less frequently, that he was the greatest architect ever to have lived. Not everyone would place him in this exalted position but one would have to ponder deeply to come up with an alternative.

One of the factors that has inhibited the proper appreciation of Wright's achievement is that the unbuilt works are easily forgotten among the plethora of those that were. Since the greater number of these were domestic, part of the misapprehension of his true status arises from regarding him primarily as a house builder, with Falling Water his great masterpiece. For this reason, more than usual emphasis has been placed in this book on his visionary projects or unexecuted commissions and when these are considered in isolation the power of his imagination and creative vitality can better be seen.

Another significant factor may also obscure full appreciation. He lived for a very long time, creatively motivated to the end. Of course, this gave him old master status as well as causing him to be regarded as a living legend, accolades which he may not have exactly discouraged. But in many ways these things did him no favours. If your first recognized work of importance occurs in a previous century it tends to encourage the view that what you do in a subsequent century must be old hat. And this certainly applied to Wright who was regarded by the 1930s as a spent force, a view

almost universally canvassed in Europe. Then came Falling Water and the Johnson Wax Building, later the Guggenheim Museum. Words were eaten but by this time an alternative – what may be called the Miesian scene – had arrived, and Wright acquired the dismissive 'eccentric genius' soubriquet. Till less became a bore; that is until the International Style was attacked as an inadequate long-term solution. As already noted, it was Robert Venturi who was one of the initiators of the architectural discontent and it is interesting to note that one of his early designs, his house for his mother, owes an acknowledged debt to Wright's Prairie Style.

The Wasmuth publications of 1910 and 1911 made a considerable impact on a significant number of younger European architects who, despite the common 19th-century view of American society, which regarded her culture as young and developing rather than mature and well established, recognized in Wright an inspiring humanism, a sense of organic identity with the natural world, a feeling for materials and, most significantly, an absence of dogma. This does not,

of course, mean a lack of certainty or sense of authority but does reflect the inflexibility of early-century architectural thinking.

It is therefore important to consider the actual rather than perceived significance of Wright in the developing architectural scene in Europe between the Wars. All the modern art movements of the first decades of this century that encompassed an architectural element – notably Cubism, Futurism and De Stijl, but also including some Russian input, owed a considerable and acknowledged debt to Wright's individualism which eventually provided an exciting alternative to the Machine Age aesthetic emerging from the Bauhaus of Gropius and Mies van der Rohe. The variety of architects so influenced, from Robert van t'Hoff to Carlo Scarpa, is so wide that it is not possible to widen the survey to include them here.

And the influence continues. Wright's own evaluation of his work – perceptive and hardheaded, if one reads his writings carefully – may well turn out to be that of future generations in a higher humanitarian society.